The Christian Family in Changing Times

The Christian Family in Changing Times

The Myths, Models, and Mystery of Family Life

Robert M. Hicks

Published by Baker Books
a division of Baker Book House Company
P.O. Box 6287, Grand Rapids, MI 49516-6287

Printed in the United States of America

Library of Congress Cataloging-in-Publication Data

Hicks, Robert, 1945–
The Christian family in changing times : the myths, models, and mystery of family life / Robert M. Hicks.
p. cm.
Includes bibliographical references.
ISBN 0-8010-6365-5 (pbk.)
1. Family—Religious aspects—Christianity. 2. Family—Biblical teaching. I. Title.
BT707.7 .H53 2001
261.8′3585—dc21 2001035487

For current information about all releases from Baker Book House, visit our web site:

http://www.bakerbooks.com

To my mother
Ermagene Virginia Hicks

Contents

Preface

A Time to Rethink Family

I've been married more years than I was single. I've been a father more years than without kids. So why is it at my age I feel more incompetent, unsure, and less knowledgeable about family matters than ever before? Don't get me wrong; I love my family and I'm not sure I would know who I am without them. But some days I'm just tired; not tired of my family, but tired from much of what life has thrust upon us.

I remember a time when it was difficult to find a book on the Christian family, reading on family life was non-existent, marriage enrichment and parenting seminars were still in their infancy, Christian radio rarely addressed family problems or hardly mentioned marriage issues, and Christian television had yet to be born. But today Christians are inundated with a plethora of resources available on CD ROM, audio tapes, video, web sites, Christian television, and, of course, radio. In fact, Christian broadcasting regularly addresses family issues now and has created thriving personality cults of airwave heroes.

So why another book on the family? And what has almost three decades of focusing on the family brought us? To raise the very question is to approach criticizing a tenet of the Christian faith. Yet, after three decades of intensive family teaching, one would think our families would be healthier, be better off, and have some impact on the culture around us.

In actuality, the reverse is true. Drastic changes have occurred in American families since the 1970s.[1] It's like what a law enforcement officer friend told me about crime rates: "There is a direct relation between the increase of policemen on the streets and the increase in crime statistics," he observes. The same seems to be true for the family. The more resources we throw at families, the more the family has eroded and changed for the worse. Perhaps, then, it's time to rethink the evangelical sound bite we call the "Christian family."

When we hear these words we think we know what they mean, but further probing results only in more clichés. Pick someone in your church and ask him or her to define the term *justification.* We hear that word all the time in sermons and may have some vague understanding of its relation to the "work of Christ" (another evangelical sound byte). But how many understand and appreciate its theological significance? Probably very few.

So the term "Christian family" functions like designer "clothes" on a naked emperor. To speak the truth and admit the emperor has no clothes will not engender warm feelings. But outsiders, unaware of the conspiracy of silence, will find the situation self-evident: The emperor is naked indeed! To admit Christian families do not evidence what we say we believe in is like proclaiming the emperor naked!

A caveat is in order, however. I do not in any way delight in the current state of family life in America, Christian or not. As an evangelical believer, I hold firmly to the historic Christian faith as expressed in the Apostles' Creed and the Westminster Catechism. Personally, I am a committed biblicist holding to the Bible as the final and sole authority for my faith. Theologically, I am a fan of the *Insti-*

tutes of the Christian Religion by John Calvin and have a growing appreciation for the writings of St. Augustine and Thomas Aquinas.

I say these things up front because I know some will read the things I say in this book as the raving opinions of an unregenerate. They are not. I'm born again, saved, and a believer in the finished work of Christ, the eternal purposes of God, fallen humanity, the second coming, and the virgin birth. I also have the mind of an honest inquirer and researcher. I believe sincere faith can coexist with honest inquiry into what is right and true.

For much of my life, I thought faith and inquiry should not be in conflict. But beginning with my doctoral research on family health, I began to reevaluate what I had been taught about the Christian family in light of current research. If anything, research only confirmed my biblical value system. However, a sociological study done on Christian families revealed a glaring gap between the role of "Christian" mythologies or models and clear biblical instructions. Many of the families I've studied would espouse one set of values as foundational to their concept of the family while living a different set of values. Their confessional values were based on what they thought was biblical or "Christian," while the actual functioning of their family experience was far different.

Let me illustrate this conflict. I once took a survey of couples in an evangelical Sunday school class—"Marrieds with Small Children." When I asked, "Do you believe both parents of small children should be employed?" the overwhelming response was 85 percent negative. Later, when I asked how many couples had home businesses that involved both spouses, I received a positive reply at 67 percent. More than half the number of respondents who believed it was wrong for both parents of small children to be employed were in fact working in home businesses. Personally, I have no problem with the financial reality these couples face or their practical choices, but I do have concern about the apparent discrepancy between "confessed beliefs" and "practice."

Apparently, beliefs about having a nonworking parent at home are undermined by financial realities. Or, perhaps, those surveyed responded with what they believed was the Christian community's biblical expectation while holding to an entirely different belief, one that would enable them to pay their bills. Believing that confessional commitments should make a difference in one's life, I began to explore the idea more closely. I set out to see how operational myths may fill in the gaps where the Bible is silent, or even erode the power of clear biblical injunctions.

I personally hold to the position that parents of small children should spend as much time with their children as is practical. The reason I believe this, however, is not so much based on biblical evidence but because it is a developmental necessity for mother-child/father-child bonding to take place, and it is just plain common sense. Young women are encouraged by the apostle Paul to love their husbands, love their children, and be busy at home[2] (Titus 2:4–5), but the woman in Proverbs 31 seems actively engaged in far more than just her home. What she does in buying a field and planting a vineyard (apparently a business venture) she does for the benefit of her home, while not neglecting the needy outside her home (Prov. 31:15–20). The Proverbs 31 woman is engaged in the totality of life. Should we set her against the admonition of Paul or take our pick as to which model we like best? That doesn't seem to be a valid principle of biblical interpretation. I'd rather allow both passages of Scripture to stand authoritatively and to argue for a common ground without reducing or redefining the message of either.

My own beliefs have not been distilled without personal bias. As a writer and researcher I am not immune to my own experience. During the development of this book I was dealing with my own issues of marriage and family. I faced the realization that some of the things I'd been taught in the early days did not produce what I thought God promised in his Word. At times, I found marriage and family life not to be the blessing projected at marriage seminars but a daily, ugly confrontation with myself. Disillusionment, depression, anger, and frustration often won the day in my own life. Worse, I often taught on marriage and family, communicating one thing from my notes, while entertaining serious doubts about what I was imparting to my listeners. I clung to the scriptural promise that God's Word will not return void (Isa. 55:11). I thought, *If I can just stick to Scripture and not my own feelings or experience, then the Lord will honor my teaching.* I have no idea how the Lord looks upon this conflict or my rationalization (I pray he is very gracious), but the process did lead me to examine common ideas and myths. "We don't understand life any better at fifty than at twenty," someone once observed, "but at least at fifty we know it and admit it!"

The writing process often takes interesting side roads, and I don't want to miss Robert Frost's "road not taken." So hang in there with me and journey along for the sheer intrigue of exploring new territory. If we are searching for an image of the ideal family, then, Lord willing, we will at least learn something about ourselves and our false conceptions of Christian family life, and we may gain a new appreciation for Scripture. My prayer is that each of us will be made better for the trip.

1

So What Changed about Family Life?

As I write, my wife is at work where she labors from 7:00 in the morning to around 3:00 in the afternoon. My adult son is asleep because his course of study requires labs from 1:00 to 5:00 in the morning.[1] One of my daughters works full-time and is single and raising a daughter. My other daughter is married, a mother, and with her husband serves as a Boys Town houseparent to five teenage boys. My son-in-law is responsible for giving guidance and care to these young men while being a father and husband.

And then there is me! I write, working out of our home; I maintain our yard and pool; and I do the grocery shopping and whatever else is on the list my wife leaves me in the morning. I also do adjunct teaching at a couple of institutions, speak at conferences and seminars, am active in several volunteer organizations, and serve as a chaplain in the Air National Guard.

Our family is anything but the traditional model I once thought was ideal for Christians. I could say our lives are the exception rather than the rule, but national statistics and my neighborhood paradigm suggest otherwise.

On my city block there are only five homes where small children are present. Of those only two mothers are full-time stay-at-home moms, one works full-time, and two part-time. All the fathers work full-time (which makes me the only house-husband on the block). This slice of life reflects the statistics, and while my single daughter lives in an enclave of duplexes where not one married mother is home with small children, these examples reflect the reality of middle-class neighborhoods in Orlando, Florida. I'm sure that more economically disadvantaged areas reflect even less of what has generally been thought of as "traditional families."

If research by George Barna is correct, only 20 percent of American families fit the traditional family definition of the husband as sole provider and the wife stay-at-home nurturer of their biological children.[2] These statistics are debated by James Dobson and Gary Bauer, who claim U.S. Department of Labor statistics reflect 41 percent in this category. But on the other end of the political spectrum, Senator Pat Schroeder claims only 7.1 percent of American families fit the traditional family model.[3] Either way, if the traditional family is defined by biological relations between children and husband and wife functioning in predetermined roles, we are talking about a small minority of the American population. Furthermore Barna's research does not reflect how many stay-at-home moms are in fact operating a business from home to realize additional income[4] from direct marketing, telephone or computer work, making and selling crafts, and other creative activities.

Data from the 2000 Census confirms these changes. For the first time in history, nuclear families dropped below 25 percent of American households. In fact, married couples with children under eighteen represent only 23 percent of American households, while those headed by single mothers accounted for 7 percent, rising 25 percent in the last ten years. Furthermore, 9 percent of all couple households are cohabitating unmarried couples. One-third of all households are composed of adults living alone or with people unrelated to each other. People are marrying later (the median age is now twenty-seven for men and twenty-five for women), and while divorce rates have leveled, a higher number of divorced singles are choosing not to remarry.[5] In short, the Census reflects "how complex American families are becoming."[6] It is in this complexity that we are called to live out biblical values.

Many cultural factors have brought about these changes. Corporate America has "downsized," "right-sized," and created many new "career advancement" opportunities for its workers.[7] In addition, the entire nature of work has changed. No longer is work defined as a place where someone goes to earn a living. With faxes, cell phones, beepers, and PC's, work is wherever you want it to be. Now, it's literally possible to work at any hour of the day from almost any place on the globe. This means the line between work and home has become fuzzy. Businesses now have day care facilities and homes have offices.

These social and economic changes have forced us to reevaluate men's and women's roles. Christian men now ask probing questions like, Am I no longer the head of my household because I stay at home and my wife fights the bumper to bumper traffic every day? Does the fact that she earns more money than I do make a statement about who is in charge? What does it really mean to "be in charge?" Do these things even matter to God? How much should they matter to me, my friends and relatives, or people in the church?

In addition, an increasing pluralization of American culture has taken place. Competing philosophies and lifestyles mixed with commercialization have made most of us spoiled consumers—even in how we worship and approach the idea of church. When I go to the grocery store there are over twenty different brands of coffee, and so it is when I want to select a church: Let's see, do I want church-lite or church-regular today? Do I want services on Saturday night, Sunday morning, or Sunday night? What about brand names? Well, there's Charismatic, Reformed, Dispensationalist, and Independent. Do I want to be Baptist, Presbyterian, Episcopalian, or Catholic? Do I want to sing Scripture choruses, the old hymns of the faith, or have someone entertain me with a professional performance? Decisions, decisions! The reality is that we can choose the kind of faith and worship experience we like. How much of this shopping mentality spills over in our search for a better family life?

It is time to do some serious rethinking about how the Christian family fits into our not-so-brave new world. If your home is anything like mine, we fight a daily battle trying to hold on to the importance of family, trying to live by biblical standards, and trying to live in a culture with constant change. Postmodern pressures make the concept of biblical faithfulness somewhat confusing. As the title of a best-selling book captures, we are trying to create a Christian family life in our "Little House on the Freeway." At times traffic blows by us so fast it is alarming; at other times, we sit bumper to bumper, irritated and fuming.

When you think of the phrase "Christian family," what is it that comes to your mind? In your search for the ideal family, how do you picture it? Is your image a biblical expression or merely one you *believe* to be a biblical norm? Possibly, your mental image is rooted in cultural models from one particular time and place. It may be a purely romantic notion based on personal needs and desires. It may be rooted in the way you were raised or not raised. Your image may be based on someone else's family life that seems happier than yours, for jealousy creates dissatisfaction and thinking there is something wrong with what you're experiencing.

Whatever your image of "family," I want to ask, Is your concept a healthy one? Is it workable or even possible in today's culture? Might there be several models of healthy family life, and as well, several unhealthy ones? What is family health anyway? In our search for a family ideal, have we created a family mythology that doesn't exist?

I want to make an attempt at processing biblical and historical data through the grid of inquiry. Whatever model of family life we may have embraced, we need to know where it originated. For some, that means finding out that cherished ideals about family may not be true. This is disconcerting at first, but the dispelling of myths proves illuminating and freeing; some have called it a second conversion. I promise you will at least be challenged, stretched, and hopefully illuminated.

2

How Hollywood Taught Me to Think about Family

"Family defines us . . . family of origin."

When the word *family* is thrown at me, I think first of my family of origin. "Family defines us, leaving its imprint on every aspect of our character," observes author and editor Rodney Clapp. "It is the earliest and most indelible 'world' we know."[1] That's why a personal family experience is probably the most determinative teacher of all.

The "Ideal" Family I Grew Up In

My father's parents left their Missouri farm while he was still young and moved to a city in a neighboring state. Dad dropped out of school in the eighth grade in order to help support his family and make his own money, saving enough money to take flying lessons. He worked for Montgomery Ward loading trucks. At that time Wichita, Kansas, was considered the air capital of the world and there were plenty of veteran World War I pilots offering rides and lessons on the weekends. Dad obtained a license to fly even before he had a driver's license.

One summer, a young lady moved next door to my father's home. She was a farm girl, come to spend the summer with city relatives. Mom attended Friends University in Wichita until money got short; she then trained as a hairstylist, working full-time until she married my father.

Dad went to work at the Travel Air airplane factory after they grew tired of him hanging around on weekends. He'd wash planes, push planes in and out of hangars, hand out flyers for weekend biplane rides, and serve as a "go-for" when anyone gave him something to do. During this time, he came to know two of aviation's greatest pioneers, Clyde Cessna and Walter Beech. When Travel Air closed its doors because of the Depression, Beech took a handful of employees and started Beech Aircraft; Dad left his day job to become their first accountant. He was also involved in the construction of Beech's first plane, the Model 17 Staggerwing.[2]

During World War II my father, who was already in the Air Corps, desperately wanted to fly in combat. The Army, however, wanted only single men for the extremely hazardous duty of piloting airplanes in wartime. They accepted him for a desk job but not for flying and recommended he stay civilian and support the war effort by continuing to build aircraft.

It was during these war years that Beech Aircraft was put on the map. This gave my father the opportunity to demonstrate his management abilities. By the end of the war, Dad, with an eighth-grade education, played a significant role in developing the new sleek, low-wing, V-tailed Bonanza that became the standard for private aviation.[3]

As children came along, my mother stayed at home to be homemaker and mother of three. Fortunately, Dad earned an income that made this possible. They built a house in one of the new subdivisions on the outskirts of Wichita, where my sisters and I lived out our childhood and adolescence. My formative years during the 1950s were that of the classic, traditional American family, as were most of my friends'. What is most intriguing is I don't remember our family ever being called "biblical" or "Christian." Our next door neighbors were a Jewish doctor's family who didn't live differently than we, except they went to synagogue instead of to church.[4] They put up Christmas trees and exchanged presents with us, and I was usually jealous that they got two holidays, Hanukkah and Christmas. The point is, I was not conscious of some ideal form of family my parents were trying to pull off. Everyone was just doing what they needed to do to provide the financial and emotional resources needed to support a growing family.

I do remember going to some kids' homes and finding it strange that their mothers weren't at home during the day. At the time, I didn't know what social classes were. Now I know those homes were less economically advantaged.

Beech Aircraft was booming in both the civilian and military markets; as a result Dad was asked to promote and relocate to Herrington, Kansas, where they could produce military trainers. Our family took a trip to Herrington and my mother wept! Everything from schools to housing was a real step backward. Dad turned down the offer but was then asked to commute. Certainly, he answered, but not by car. The offer came back, "Go out to the line and make yourself a plane."[5] As a result, during most of my junior high years, Dad lived in the Herrington Hotel and flew home Wednesday nights and on weekends. Some of my greatest memories are climbing up on top of our house and looking for my father on the horizon. When I saw the distinctive V-tailed Bonanza "buzz" the house and move its wings from side to side, I would run into the house and tell my mom it was time to go pick up Dad.

Now I wonder if during the period my dad commuted, were we no longer a traditional family? I know I missed having my dad at home. I know he greatly regretted missing so much of my adolescence.[6] I still look at my parents as two people just trying to do the best they could for their family. But is there anything more biblical about the way I was raised compared to my less economically advantaged childhood friends? My wife's background, also, was radically different from mine. She experienced frequent geographical moves plus stepfather and half-sister relationships. Does this make her family experience less ideal, or less Christian?

The Power of Myth

No matter what our family experiences have been, they take on the power of imparting meaning where meaning may be lacking. In scholarly literature, such power is called "myth." The word *myth* in this sense is not used to refer to something that isn't true or doesn't have a real existence, but to something that provides significance or rationale. Myths help us understand and make sense of complex issues and experiences under the guise of some image or model. In family studies and family therapy, finding the mythologies that guide our personal thinking and decision-making is axiomatic to the field.[7] We all have them but usually are not aware of them.

Next to the power of personal experience, the greatest purveyor of myths is the media. In ancient cultures the power of story played that role. In the twentieth century, stories came alive in three dimensions on TV and in movies. The power of media images on our concept of family is powerful.

The Victorian Myth

What comes to your mind when you think of Victorian England? Well, it depends on your exposure to the history of that period and its representation in novels, films, and television programs. One image that comes to my mind is that of Mary Poppins. The home where Mary is to work reflects a family organization where the husband is protector and provider of the family. His wife is the domestic manager of the household and supervisor of the children's education and social training. The father's attitude toward children was they were "to be seen but not heard." Children were not to be viewed as adults until they were properly trained and/or married. Much of the Victorian wife's virtue and success was judged by the sterling character and performance of her children. The husband's virtue and success was judged by his performance and the esteem granted from the world of business. This family belonged in the upper-middle class of the landed gentry, owned a large house complete with servants, and had enough money to hire a full-time nanny.

This image begs an important question. How many families during Victorian England are represented in this image? The image may be true, but for how many? One of the problems we have in understanding the family from any historical period is that the field of family studies is a new discipline.[8] It wasn't until the early 1950s that degree programs were offered in family studies. For most of history the family was not a subject of scholarly inquiry. Researchers are dependent upon diaries, letters to spouses, and legal documents (mostly divorce cases and property transfers). Literacy often excludes how the poor and uneducated peasants lived.[9] The best of history is always limited to someone's access to data, so knowing how one group lived is not the same as knowing how everyone lived. One researcher noted, "No two families, no two lives, can possibly be the same, let alone a hundred, or a thousand, or a million. The task, therefore, is finding the 'central tendency.'"[10]

Just as my experience in the 1950s was radically different from some of my friends', so the image of Victorian

England assumed in Mary Poppins may be no more than a mythology. To balance out this mythology, let's place another image into the mix. If we consider Charles Dickens's *A Christmas Carol* and look more at the character Bob Cratchet than at Ebenezer Scrooge, we get a glimpse of a different reality. If you remember, Cratchet is the struggling assistant who tries to support his family, including a handicapped son, with no servants. Scrooge unjustly takes advantage of Crachet's labor in order to make himself wealthier. The social conditions of England were such that the life of Cratchet may be more characteristic of families than that of Mary Poppins.

Victorian England represents the triumph of British imperialism, capitalism, and industrialization during the nineteenth century. It was a time when household production gave way to wage work and occupations outside the home. A strict division of labor by gender emerged, defining women's roles as "domestics" and men's as "breadwinners." But the economic success of some (a minority) was often at the expense of others, who suffered degrading human experiences in coal mines and factories.

Stephanie Coontz writes, "The Victorian middle-class family depended for its existence on the multiplication of other families who were poor and powerless to retreat into their own little oases, and who therefore had to be the provision of the oases of others. . . . By 1820 'half of the workers in factories were boys and girls who had not reached their eleventh birthday.'"[11]

At the turn of the century (Queen Victoria died in 1901), one-third of the population of London, the world's richest city, was living in poverty.[12] In the United States during the same period, 120,000 children worked in Pennsylvania coal mines and factories, and in Scranton, Pennsylvania, one-third of girls aged thirteen to sixteen worked in silk mills. By the turn of the century, 24 percent of the Southern states' textile workforce was children.[13] Without child labor laws, industry regulations, minimum wage, or worker's rights, the Victorian age was anything but ideal, except for an elitist few. An interesting note is that it was during this time the entire field of psychology was born in Freud's research of middle-class women. John Demos observes, "Freud's early patients were composed of troubled women from the 'comfortable classes' of the late Victorian period."[14]

In spite of the historical reality, it is easy for evangelical Christians to envision this period as a time when the ideal family was alive and well. In truth, the family model is nothing more than the typical bourgeois family, strictly rooted in the upper-middle-class economic and social values of the period. There was nothing uniquely Christian about it.

For every Victorian middle-class family protecting and providing for its children within the family circle, there was probably an Irish or German girl scrubbing the floors, a Welsh boy shoveling coal into the furnace, an African girl doing the laundry, and an Italian child working in a sweat shop making dresses for the lady of the house! Therefore, a "Christian" substantiation for this model as ideal is doubtful. The concepts that men should be the sole money managers or that women are too fragile to do physical labor are soundly rooted in the upper-middle-class values of Victorian England. In the lower classes, women did much of the physical labor while many men spent the family livelihood at local pubs. In reality these divisions of labor by gender have little to do with the Bible or the physical and mental abilities of male or female. They have more to do with social standing. If I expect my wife to "attend" to the children because I think that's her role, I may have this Victorian image in my mind. Likewise, if she assumes my sole responsibility is to pay the bills, she might be influenced by Victorian thinking about the family.

The Colonial Puritan Myth

During my seminary years, some fellow classmates became enamored with the Puritans. They read everything they could get about them, especially New England Puritans. One evening my wife and I were invited to dinner at the home of one of these Puritan devotees. After dinner, the mother put to bed a couple of their children, and my wife went along to take a tour of the house. When she came back she noted with a little shock that their small children slept in the same room with the parents. (Yes, the house had more than one bedroom.) Our host responded with a lengthy theological and historical justification. He had read somewhere about Puritans sleeping with their children in order to enhance their emotional security and feelings of safety. Since our host was one of those who felt this particular period in American history was the most "spiritual," he explained that they intended to emulate their literary mentors in every way.

On the way home my wife commented, " I don't think I want you to read the Puritans!"

I find Americans in particular are always looking for hidden secrets to a successful life. Look at the sales statistics of the "success" literature, all promising to reveal the "secrets" of successful companies, leadership, entrepreneurship, and even family life. For our friends, the "secret" was tucked away in Puritan America, where the simple practice of a few, or the common practice of keeping children warm during cold New England nights, became a myth.

The practice is reminiscent of a newly wedded wife preparing her first roast beef. Her husband, watching the preparations, noticed she cut off both ends of the roast before placing them into the pan. When he asked her why she does this, she replied, "That's the way my mother did it." The young wife was puzzled, however, by the question and asked her mother why she always cut the ends off a roast. Her mother explained, "Well dear, that's what your grandmother always did." The young bride, still not satisfied, called her aging grandfather in a nursing home and asked, "Why did Grandmother always cut off the ends of a roast?" He answered, "Oh, because we never had a pan large enough." This is how historical experience takes on mythological power!

The Puritan myth illustrates the power one generational experience has on another generation.[15] Don't get me wrong. I love New England's white clapboard churches with bell towers and quaint cemeteries nestled into town squares. They speak of a time when things were better. Snow-covered valleys and scenes of families snuggled into horse-drawn sleighs bring back romantic images of a slower, less stressful time. Fresh snow falling on the sleigh that is taking a family to church is the classic image of the picture-postcard beauty of New England. Certainly, the colonial period of American history was determinative politically and spiritually for the United States. But was it, in fact, the way we think it was? Was family life back then the way family life is supposed to be?

A well-known Puritan, Jonathan Edwards, studied twelve hours a day and took long afternoon walks, during which he collected and documented the flora and fauna of New England. Edwards rarely visited the families in his parish but spent most of his time praying, writing, and reading. When I pastored a small church, I tried to sell my board on this schedule, obviously a spiritual one since Edwards is remembered as one of the most intelligent and influential characters of the period. My brothers in the faith, however, were not as impressed as I. Hospital calls, counseling, staff and elder meetings were all requirements of my job. I quickly realized there was no way I could implement a Puritan schedule in my pastorate. The pastoral world of Jonathan Edwards and the "running through airports" world of the twentieth century are in two different universes. My conclusion is the same about family life.

The colonial New England period of the Puritans *was* very Christian (some might say too Christian). But in what sense was it Christian? For whom, and for how long? How much of Puritan family life was determined by socioeconomic issues? Did their faith dictate a certain structure? Demos notes, "People of that time and culture did not have a particularly self-conscious orientation to family life . . . family life was something they took largely for granted."[16]

It is easy to take long walks enjoying the botanical elements of nature and to study Scripture all day when someone else is paying the bill. But I wonder about how shopkeepers lived and what life was like for indentured servants during the same period. Records indicate that for many who had fallen into debt, the only option was to sell their lives to property owners until the debt was worked off. Also, in some communities, 30 to 40 percent of all brides were pregnant at the altar. And it was common for magistrates to compel "fighting" couples to "live in peace" by threatening to take their children away if they didn't! In fact, a Massachusetts Assembly ordered that any child over the age of six who had not learned the alphabet could be removed to another family.[17] By the end of the Puritan period popular literature reflected complaints about divorce, desertion, and women being restless in their homemaker role.[18] Apparently Puritanism was not conducive to ideal family life for everyone.

Puritan family structure was not as we have pictured it. The basic unit was the nuclear family with a husband, wife, and children. However, nonbiologically related family members were also common. Non-kin included a variety of orphans, apprentices, hired laborers, and foster children. Add to these the regular household servants and at times convicts and "indigents," and we have a family structure that some have called a "lively representation" of the community at large. In fact, without government assistance the church/family relationship functioned as the social welfare net for the community.[19]

It is easy to conclude that Puritan America was Christian simply because everyone went to church. But why did they go to church? Were there serious repercussions for not attending church? What if they did not attend the dominant Congregational Church? Would they suffer economically or be ostracized from the community? Yale historian Sydney Ahlstrom records, "For the first time in Christendom, a state church with vigorous conceptions of enforced uniformity in belief and practice was requiring an internal, experiential test [that of offering some visible evidence of regenerating grace] of church membership." He concludes, "Many future problems in New England churches stemmed from this decision."[20]

It is far easier to hang on to romantic notions about the period rather than recognize that Puritan New England was not free from the vices, sins, and religious conflicts that characterized other periods of American history. Ahlstrom notes, "The New England Zion was never an untroubled Christian utopia. Settlement brought unsettlement."[21] Around 1670 Puritans began distilling molasses into rum, which eventually replaced hard cider and home-brewed beer as the drink of the country. American rum trade began when the Puritans found great demand for their New England products in the West Indies. Samuel Eliot Morison observes, "This West Indies trade was the main factor in New England prosperity until the American Revolution . . . without it [rum trade] the settlements on the northern coast would have remained stationary or declined."[22] This portion of Puritan history is conveniently ignored by many evangelicals. Another little-known fact about this period is that more alcoholism was reported than in any other period of American history! Does this mean there were Christian drunks, or were these alcohol abusers only non-Christians? What was the impact of alcohol abuse on wives and children?

And what about the famous Salem witch trials? No matter what one believes about capital punishment, how Christian was it to execute women by burning them at the stake? Demos observes, "Women in their middle years were more likely to run afoul of official norms" than younger women. This turning against the norms brought charges of witchcraft, where the average age of the accused was over forty.[23]

If we believe the secret to successful family life lies in getting back to New England Puritanism, we are in trouble, trying to turn a myth into reality. It won't work. The romanticizing of any period of history is lethal to truth. My view about the Puritan period is that there were many godly men and women during the time and many ungodly ones. That's the nature of the gospel in today's world. The Puritans had their unique problems. It was not the ideal Christian community often portrayed by politicians and preachers. Just as today, wheat and weeds grow together until Jesus comes back to make a just separation (Matt. 13:24–30).

The Frontier Myth

I call nostalgic impressions about frontier America's family life The Little House on the Prairie model. I remember when the television series by that name began its long run. It was a refreshing change from the seventies quiz shows and sitcoms. *Dallas* was the rage at that time, so anything would have been an improvement, but *Little House* episodes held our family captive with riveting plots and intense character development. For younger readers or any who may not know what I'm talking about, let me describe the

Ingalls family, whose television version pictured homesteading at the turn of the century on the Kansas plains. The series depicted the values of an idealized farmer against extreme odds. Father Ingalls is shown as the strong head of the household, braving the challenges of earning a living and raising a family on the plains. The Ingallses have a loving marriage and three little girls, a family who faces the conflicts of harsh winters, unreasonable people, and crises of faith. *Little House on the Prairie* achieved award-winning drama.

My daughters grew up during the run of *Little House*, and we enjoyed watching the Ingallses' church life portrayed in a healthy manner. It was hard not to watch one episode without identifying personally with someone or something in the situation development. In many ways, the Ingalls family was the kind of family we all wished we could have been (except we'd want a bigger, more comfortable house near a city). The loyalty, compassion, and commitment of the Ingallses to each member of their family was the kind of stuff that brought tears to the eye.

Except, wait a minute! Where was I raised? In Kansas! I had studied Kansas history as a requirement in both elementary and secondary schools. One day it finally dawned on me that the *Little House on the Prairie* I saw dramatized on television was far removed from the prairie history I learned as a child. Again, the history of the Ingalls family in novel form may be an accurate accounting of one family's life, but how true was it for the majority of prairie families?[24]

During the Civil War, the territory of Kansas was called "bloody Kansas" because blood was spilled on the key issue of slavery. Northern Kansas was abolitionist while southern Kansas was pro-slavery. The Mason-Dixon Line ran directly through the middle of Kansas, the only state with this distinction. The division made for some of the bloodiest nonmilitary violence in the war.

After the Civil War, there were opportunities for newcomers to stake a claim in Kansas in order to try to eke out a living off the land. Many of these homesteaders were Confederate soldiers who couldn't go back to their states of origin (for things they had done in the war), criminals, and some who came in the interest of owning their first piece of property.[25] Many of these early land-grant prairie farms failed. Settlers who stayed to raise crops soon found themselves at odds with the cattle industry. Bloody battles ensued between farmers and cattlemen driving their herds along the historic Chisholm Trail to the stockyards and trains in Wichita. Farmers' fences prohibited these drives, so relations between farmers and cattlemen were anything but cooperative.

Periodic conflicts with local Native American tribes were also common. And these were also the times of Jesse James, Wyatt Earp, and Doc Holiday. The rule of law was established in many frontier towns by gunslingers turned lawmen who could outdraw any opponent. Wichita, where I was raised, was divided by the Arkansas River. During its early history (1880s) the east side of town was where the good, church-going, Christian people lived. The west side was the domain of taverns, whiskey, gambling, and prostitutes. One early historian coined the phrase, "No god west of the Arkansas."[26] A bridge to connect the two sides of town was hotly debated for years on the argument that it would give opportunity to corrupt the young. Even when I was in high school, the west side image still had these overtones. But today, my mother lives there, and it is one the fastest-growing areas of the city. In fact, you can now buy liquor on both sides of the Arkansas!

I'm sure there were probably some prairie families like the Ingalls family on the frontier, but how many, and at what period of time? Certainly, the TV series did an admirable job in making the Ingalls family's life the envy of many Americans, but perhaps it is for the most part mythology, offering good feelings about how families ought to be. The concept of self-reliant families conquering the elements should be moderated by the reality that many prairie farmers owed their existence to federal land grants and government-funded military outposts protecting them while dispossessing thousands of Native American families from their lands. Historian Patricia Nelson Limerick writes, "Territorial experience got Westerners in the habit of federal subsidies."[27]

But the myth of the rugged father taking on the frontier with no outside help dies hard. One of the most difficult decisions I had to make as a husband and father was "lowering" myself to accept food stamps. In graduate school and working part-time, I felt that to accept government aid was humiliating and a genuine sign of my failure as economic provider. I did not want my wife in the grocery line paying with food stamps. When we met with the government office, they looked at our situation and quickly said, "You are the kind of people the program is designed for. We know this is only temporary for you, and you will be paying into the system the rest of your lives." I concluded they were right. I wonder how many other evangelical conservatives are out there who believe government subsistence is wrong or misused while having been beneficiaries of government school loans, GI Bills, Medicare, or food stamps?

The Depression-Era Myth

During the 1970s *The Waltons* provided powerful television images of family life during the Depression era. The family included Mom, Dad, kids, grandparents, grandchildren, and a few other distressed extended family members to boot. The house was depicted as a beehive of activity, and with seven kids there was always something that became the focus of an episode. Mother Walton carried the genuine, warm-hearted Christian faith. Father Walton's faith was more personal, reserved, and, at times, doubtful. He usually appeared nonreligious, but tolerant of church and of his wife's faith. John Boy, the storyteller and oldest in the family, was the chronicler of the Walton adventures.

The message this family image held was that of a family doing whatever they could to survive the Depression and keep their extended family together. In contrast to the frontier independence myth, the Waltons survived through the multiple resources of extended family, the larger community, and sometimes strangers. It is similar to the stories my mother told. She milked cows, cut off heads of chickens, cultivated a working vegetable garden, and sold pies to anyone who had money to buy them. My grandfather often put unemployed men to work on the farm so they might have food for their families. Granddad paid them in chickens, eggs, fruits, vegetables, or whatever he had.

But how does this family match up to the reality of other families during the time? Glen Elder records, "Depression families evoke nostalgia in some contemporary observers." However, he says the reality was "a corrosive and disabling poverty that shattered the hopes and dreams of young parents and twisted the lives of those who were 'stuck together' in it."[28] What the Walton myth creates is an expectation for families to survive with support of extended family and community. Though times were bad, the scene is that of a rural, pastoral haven where one family survived based on shared commitment and supportive love. The message is what we are all looking for and perhaps the way we wish our families could be. But what was the reality for those living in city squalors? Without jobs, family, money, or opportunities, their experience was far different. The Depression migration from small towns and family farms to population centers placed many in poverty.

My mother confessed that living on a farm made her family better off than those living unemployed in the city during the Great Depression. In urban centers, families had to double or triple up in crowded apartments; three-generation households increased dramatically. Many men left their families to look for work elsewhere, leaving homes abandoned to wives and children. Young boys roamed the streets of cities like Chicago and New York. Unemployed men turned to alcohol and became violent, while women filled the gaps by taking any kind of work they could. If they had out-of-work husbands they often belittled them for not being providers, and children gave up any dreams of education or escaping poverty.

Today, the rural Walton myth still exists, and certainly families *should* pull together during tough times. But shoulds do not necessarily become the way things are. When relatives live at a distance or a marriage is not working, family life is painted in radically different hues. There have been many days in my married life when I was ready to catch the first flight to the Cayman Islands or go live a solitary life in the mountains. What I've found is that the desire to flee the city for a slower, rural life is rooted in the comparison of my life to the myth. Compared to the Waltons, my life comes up short. Extended family members do not show up at my door when I am in need. Community members do not bring food. The pastor doesn't make a social call. The Bible's Book of Proverbs abounds with family realism: Sometimes a nearby friend is better than a far relative (Prov. 27:10). It is better to be single than in a contentious marriage (Prov. 21:19). These are the realities many face whether they are Christians or not.

The Urban Industrial Myth

The 1950s are best remembered by black-and-white television culture, coinciding with one of the most simultaneously stable and fearful times in American history.

Dwight Eisenhower was president for eight years, a time of unparalleled economic success, while the Soviet nuclear threat grew. I still remember the surprise bomb alerts in elementary school, where we placed our hands behind our necks and had to kneel under our desks until all-clear sirens were sounded. The Veterans Administration funded education, home purchases, and low-interest business loans. As a pro-family-values period, marriage was universally praised and a baby explosion took place. New suburban schools were built and school violence meant having a bully push you around the bicycle rack after school. Eighty-five percent of all new homes were in suburbs, where nuclear families could live out the American dream. The economic success of the period allowed working-class families like mine to move into middle-class prosperity, and what we now call the traditional family became normative, or at least we think it was.

Many have called this myth the *Leave it to Beaver* or *Father Knows Best* model of family life. Gary Bauer of the Family Research Council claims "these TV shows usually contained subtle value lessons about honesty, hard work, and commitment."[29] For years, this model had been on the horizon. Western industrialization and urbanization in both Europe and America had increasingly taken men out of the home and put them into factories, mines, and offices where they would spend most of their waking hours. This left the domain of the home entirely in the hands of women and created a separation of labor that was not known previously. For women, the home became the child-raising center and a place that demanded the domestic management of "time-saving" conveniences.

One researcher observed in the family dynamics of the 1950s "the first wholehearted effort to create a home that would fulfill virtually all its members' personal needs through an energized and expressive personal life."[30]

By the end of the decade the child-centered home was firmly at the center of the American dream. For women, a new specialty, "home economics," appeared in the school curriculum. In my junior high school there was no option; if you were a girl you took home economics while guys were required to take shop, where we learned to make generators and telegraphs, to work in sheet metal, and to operate power tools. (I liked my girlfriend's brownies but don't remember her being impressed by my generator!) What these two courses illustrate was the complete separation of roles for men and women at the time. What men did, they did in the garage where their tools were, and where they would not get the house dirty. What women did was predominately in the kitchen, and even with the labor-saving inventions of the 1950s, women's housework time actually increased as compared to both the war and pre-war years.[31]

From the perspective of the twenty-first century, I am amazed no one questioned this strict gender role stereotyping. Since I now do much of the cooking in our home, I wish I had taken a course in home economics; so far, I haven't had any need to make a generator.

Problematic about the 1950s family is that it is romanticized as the model we should get back to. If the "traditional" family existed, however, it existed for only a few. In real life, fathers didn't even exist for the child actors on *Father Knows Best.* Laurin Chapin, known as "Kitten" on the show, had an abusive father who sexually molested her, while her mother was an alcoholic who often came to the set drunk. Laurin's on-set older brother, Billy Gray, became a pot-head shortly after the program was canceled, busted on drug charges in 1962.[32] Even this ideal family was dysfunctional.

Neither was the experience of my friends that of the traditional family. There were no food stamps, and with a 25 percent poverty level, the economic plight for many families was severe. In addition, TV show families were, of course, all white Anglos, an image that did not figure in the explosion of black and Hispanic populations in the cities. African American women living in southern states did not enjoy a June Cleaver kind of life. With a 50 percent poverty rate they faced outright brutality. Coontz writes, "The happy, homogenous families that we 'remember' from the 1950s were thus partly a result of the media's denial of diversity."[33] Where problems existed they were completely denied, or glossed over. How the family *appeared* was all-important. "No one told the truth," says Benita Eilser. "People pretended they weren't unfaithful. They pretended that they weren't homosexual. They pretended that they weren't horrible." [34]

I can't number the times I heard from my parents, preachers, teachers, and coaches the phrase, "What will people think?" I ask, what people? From parents it was what other parents, the school, the church, or their friends would think. From teachers and coaches it was what parents or fellow students would think. At church it was what other Christians or church members might think. Appearances drove behavior.

Thus, the 1950s for many white middle-class families was nothing more than wiping a happy face across marital and family problems. Tranquilizers were discovered and used to mask many difficulties. What was brewing underneath the façade of happiness would explode into the radical rebellion of the late 1960s and 1970s. Women were no longer content with their middle-class lives and began to break with the imprisonment they felt. *The Feminine Mystique* by Betty Friedan touched the nerve of many women and became a best-seller. The children of "perfect" families began to act out the unexpressed pain and disillusionment of their parents, emerging as hippies, yippies, and yuppies.

Those wanting to get back to the traditional family of the '50s must realize it was not a utopian time. Where family health did thrive, the question must be asked, Was this just an aberration, a blip on the screen of American history, or a period that must be restored if we are to see our families strong again? When I hear the phrase "return to family values" I hear a longing to get back to the 1950s. But would the same people who desire to get back to this period also grant that in some ways our country might be better off today? The Soviet threat is gone, equal pay and opportunity now exist for minorities, and a powerful media keeps watch on the political process, balancing if not thwarting past abuses.

Was the 1950s more Christian than today? That is debatable. Certainly, church attendance is greater today and the percentage of those who confess belief in God has never been greater (80 to 90 percent by some polls). The myth dies hard, but what has happened in more recent history? Father no longer knows best, and it would be insane to leave it to Beaver. Evangelicals are concerned about the demise of the traditional family structure while at the same time trying to insulate children from the "decaying culture." Courses of Christian study like *Raising Children God's Way* abound.[35] Current cultural realities raise questions like, Should gay marriages be thought of as true marriages? Should gay adults be able to adopt children? If so, should they be called a family? Is "family" limited only to biological relationships or does it refer to anyone living in the same domicile? What about single parents and children or single adults who live together—are they to be considered "family?" Such are the realities the current culture has thrown into the face of the Christian church as well as Judaism and Islam.

The Great Evangelical Obsession

Are cultural realities to be viewed as the demise of the ideal family or are they merely the kind of changes that have taken place many times throughout history? Could it be that what we think of as the traditional family was just an anomaly? If our search for a perfect family form is merely a search for a phantom, what does this say about us?

What these sorts of questions illustrate is that the great fundamentalist omission (the model Christian home) during the early part of the twentieth century has turned into a great evangelical obsession. The history of the Liberal Fundamentalist controversy of the 1920s is illustrative. How the Christian family was to be defined or structured was not important to early fundamentalists, whose concern was for the orthodoxy of the faith.[36] As conservative Christians pulled out of liberal mainstream denominations, they began to build institutions and organizations that would be based on the final authority of the Bible and preserve the "fundamentals of the faith." (This included divine inspiration of the Bible, virgin birth, deity of Christ, bodily resurrection, and the second coming.) A particular view of the Christian family was not a "fundamental of the faith" and, in fact, the Christian family was rarely mentioned. This was an era when great Christian empire builders were establishing new denominations, seminaries, and mission organizations. The family was not at the center of their concern. The research I have done shows if the family was addressed at all, it was just an overlaying of Bible verses upon a particular cultural consensus.[37]

Most evangelical seminaries did not offer courses on the family until the sixties or seventies, when an explosion of them took place as baby boomers married. The institution of the family was then questioned and reexamined in both secular and Christian circles. At my seminary, Dr. Howard Hendricks began teaching one of the first courses on the Christian home. Hendricks and Rev. Tim LaHaye formed a working relationship that would result in one of the first seminars on family life in the country. From their early efforts many other organizations followed, but the pivotal impetus in redirecting the course of family life among Christians came with the publishing of *Dare to Discipline* by James Dobson. As a result of its phenomenal success followed by his other writings, Dr. Dobson left his medical school faculty position to start Focus on the Family.

The impact of Focus on the Family on the lives of evangelicals and even those outside the faith is one of the rich stories of evangelical success. When I was a young seminarian and later pastor, my wife and I cut our parental teeth on the literature, tapes, and videos authored by Dobson. Our grown children still remember the positive (and sometimes literal) impact this one individual made on our family. In my estimation Dobson is one of the great spiritual leaders of our generation. My few personal interactions with him (conversations at Family Research Council meetings) only heightened my respect and opinion of his faith and Christian character. It is therefore with deep appreciation for him as a person and his accomplishments that I share my concern about the perceived impact of Focus on the Family.

Little examination has been given to the influence Focus on the Family has had on American evangelicals. Some believe Dobson to be a heretic of the faith, or "Psycho-Heretic."[38] But these sources also call me by the same label, so I consider myself in good company. My concern for Focus on the Family is not about its spiritual fidelity, but in the realm of brotherly wisdom. Without a doubt, Dr. Dobson's quantitative impact has been great and continues to be. However, evaluating the quality of any impact is not as easy.

First of all, there is a problem even questioning this organization or its founder. From my own experience, to do so is to be placed in the category of either not being a Christian at all or questioning one of the fundamentals of the faith! My hunch is that this is not in the spirit of Dobson himself, yet there is a fear by some in the evangelical community of being blacklisted if they dare to raise a voice. As a pastor and seminary professor, I have observed at the grass-roots level that Dobson's teaching on the family often becomes equated with what is biblical. Therefore, to question one of his views is to question the Bible, according to some. There is fear within the Christian Bookseller Association of saying anything negative about Focus on the Family. Such fear serves no purpose, because no one, including this writer, is above criticism. I even have the distinction of having one of my books picketed![39]

Evangelical columnist Cal Thomas complained that Dr. Dobson was "the only one who refused to do an interview with him" for fear Thomas would be critical.[40] We all need the honest inquiry of brothers and sisters, even outsiders, to keep us balanced. My concern is that Focus on the Family has become insulated and rarely considers contrary opinions. Why is it that Focus on the Family should be questioned? Two reasons.

First, as a child psychologist Dr. Dobson's longstanding mission has been for the welfare of children and their normal development. When he first started writing (1971), evangelical opinion suspected anything that had to do with psychology.[41] There may have been Christians who were psychologists but no one embraced "Christian Psychology" as a science, for Christianity and psychology were incompatible bedfellows, it was believed. Christians distrusted psychology, and psychologists found no use for Christianity. So at the time, Dobson, being a committed believer and a professional in child development, was a breath of fresh air to many. Instruction about the nature of the child mixed with parenting advice on the subjects of discipline, nurture, and boundaries were needed from an expert within the faith. (Christians of that time had heard enough of the permissive Dr. Spock.)

What this corrective emphasis has done, however, is to portray Dobson's views on child development as biblical when they are not. I do not mean Dobson's views are unbiblical, just abiblical. The authority for many of his family opinions lies in personal anecdotes and stories rather than the Bible.

In his own words:

> The book you have been reading about the strong-willed child also contains many suggestions and perspectives which I have not attempted to validate or prove . . . the underlying principles are not my own innovative insights. Instead they originated with the inspired biblical writers. My purpose has been nothing more than to verbalize the Judeo-Christian tradition regarding discipline of children and to apply those concepts to today's families.[42]

Without offering proof for his suggestions and opinions or scriptural references, he claims his material is rooted in the Bible. However, it's clear that much of what Dobson teaches is rooted more in modern child-development theories and conservative common sense mixed with the industrial home model known as the "traditional" family.

Early Dobson publications corrected the neglect and oversight of the family by early fundamentalists and the extremes of a Spock permissiveness. But with this correction came assumptions about family life that may or may not have anything to do with biblical or evangelical Christianity. Dr. Dobson openly admits "the best source for guidance for parents is found in the wisdom of the Judeo-Christian ethic."[43] However, in the book *Dare to Discipline,* he outlines five "underpinnings for commonsense children rearing."[44] These, I agree, are all "commonsense" underpinnings, but unfortunately none of the principles of child rearing have any scriptural references. In fact, in his seminal work on child discipline, Dobson writes 247 pages of text before there is a direct reference to biblical passages. My concern is that his "commonsense" principles are under the guise of the Judeo-Christian ethic, but his documentation is from emotive stories and personal illustrations. Biblical references finally appear in the last chapter, "A Moment for Mom," under the subcategory of "Seek Divine Wisdom." Apparently, only mothers need divine wisdom!

Dr. Dobson concludes *Dare to Discipline* by saying, "From Genesis to Revelation there is a consistent foundation on which to build an effective philosophy of parent-child relationship."[45] Again, I have no difficulty with the above statement (and in fact embrace it as true); where I have the problem is that a biblical foundation was not given in the book. Commonsense principles for child raising mixed with touching stories and illustrations does not make for a biblical view of the family. Dobson doesn't cover Genesis to Revelation on the subject of the family (nor was that his task); neither does he touch on difficult biblical subjects like stoning disobedient sons, putting family members to death when they entice us to sin, or raising children of a deceased family member. These are also "family values" in the book of Deuteronomy (13:6–9; 24:5) but need to be placed into a broader context of biblical theology and family life for proper understanding. I don't expect Dobson to be an expert on Scripture since that is not his field, but I believe he does a disservice to Christian readers by claiming biblical authority for what is mostly commonsense.

In short, what Focus on the Family represents is a psychologizing of family life not that much different from other contemporary views. Again, I don't have a problem with this, only with the perception that if something is psychologically sound, or implies certain commonsense justification, it is therefore biblical. Dobson's approach to family life has more in common with what has become the urban industrial model (traditional family model) than the direct teaching of Scripture. Some have even questioned the long-term impact of child-centered philosophies on parents. Penelope Leach argues in her classic work that "a society so inimical to children . . . in fact devalues parents and makes good parenting exceedingly difficult."[46] The identification of bruises on a child or a father being too affectionate with a daughter is enough to raise accusations of abuse today. Leach argues the child-centered home has brought about these extreme views. Focusing on the family can easily gravitate to obsessing about children and pressuring parents to be "superparents," a strategy bound to fail.

The child-centered home has, in fact, not always been the case. Pre-industrial families were more marriage-centered, founded upon the necessity of being economic production centers. "The family of modern times is a historic product of the European Middle Ages," write Frances and Joseph Gies. "Prior to this time marriage was an economic enterprise and due to infant mortality, people could not allow themselves to become too attached to something that was regarded as a probable loss."[47] Affection for children existed in these families, but parents had to maintain a certain "emotional detachment" for fear of losing them. Another writer suggests, "Good mothering is an invention of modernization and among the lower classes a parental 'pattern of indifference' extended well into the nineteenth century."[48]

The writings and radio programs of James Dobson have profoundly secured the child-centered home in its urban industrial structure as "the" model of the Christian home. Parents as nurturers are held responsible for the emotional well-being of all relationships. "The bourgeois or traditional family, by contrast, has lost the family's earlier function as an economically productive unit," writes Clapp. "Its main function is sentimental. It serves as haven and oasis, an emotional stabilizer and battery-charger for its members . . . It demands that spouses and children love and trust each other, that they intensely enjoy being together."[49] In other words, couples have a significant amount of self-esteem riding on the quality of their marriage and the behavior and performance of their children. What is worse, one's spirituality is often evaluated by, if not equated to, one's quality of parenting skills and how well children turn out. What I am suggesting is that there is nothing distinctively "Christian" about this. Likewise, there is nothing necessarily "unchristian" either. It is just one way of looking at family life, a way that has become predominant.

A second concern I have about Focus on the Family is how it has become increasingly politically oriented, if not politically manipulated. I remember when Dobson served on the government's pornography commission and was shocked by what he found. We were all shocked. But this one experience, in my opinion, brought a significant change in the direction of his ministry. It seemed from that point on, the organization became increasingly aligned with right-wing politics, if not captured by their politically conservative agendas. These connections have been noted by the mainstream press but rarely acknowledged by evangelicals.[50]

Dobson's 1990 book *Children at Risk* illustrates his growing political concern. He expresses alarm over "liberal power blocks, political machinery, the American Civil Liberties Union and the American Way."[51] He calls Washington a place where "liberalism is in the saddle" and a city "controlled by an entrenched establishment firmly in the grip of an anti-family and anti-traditional family values philosophy."[52] In response to these concerns, Dobson's answer is for the reader to "counterattack" by getting involved politically. He urges, "Democracy succeeds when people get involved . . . picket, run for office, write your congressmen!"[53]

In a way, Dr. Dobson's views about family issues have become so politicized that traditional family values have taken on a sectarian partisan nature. I don't believe one's view of the family should become equated with right-wing

Republican politics, or anyone's politics for that matter. When a certain brand of Christianity or evangelicalism becomes just another special interest group banging on Washington's doors, the entire nature of Christianity is diluted. Unfortunately, in the eyes of many, Dr. Dobson is *the* voice of evangelicalism, which in turn makes him the leading voice of right-wing Republican politics. Again, this does a disservice to evangelicals, Christianity, and both political parties. Cal Thomas, in a piece titled "Focus on the Family, Not on Politics," asserted this: "Politics is about compromise and goals are mostly achieved in increments. Politics and faith are irreconcilable. The former cannot tolerate zealotry; the latter cannot tolerate compromise. This is the reason that the two, when combined, become highly combustible."[54]

Aleksandr Solzhenitsyn once observed that "one of the ironies of our times is, once certain world leaders have concluded the problems of the world are essentially spiritual, the Church has deemed their solutions to be political." I know many evangelicals who have concluded under the influence of Focus on the Family, the Family Research Council (its offspring), and the Christian Coalition that solutions to many family problems now lie in the political arena, not in the spiritual condition of the human heart.

We should all be cautioned by the evangelical, Protestant, and Catholic experience in Nazi Germany. When the Weimar Republic outlawed the German state church, Christians felt marginalized and stripped of political power. Even evangelicals felt strong political power was needed in order to deal with the deterioration of national values. The German "family values" of the Nazi party promised to deal with communists, homosexuals, and other attacks on German families. As a result, the churches joined in granting overwhelming support to the German Führer. They saw Hitler as a savior and as God-sent. Though Hitler was a pure pagan, Christians chanted, "The Swastika on our breasts, and the Cross in our hearts." Historian Paul Johnson concluded that as a result, "neither the evangelical nor the Catholic Church ever condemned the Nazi regime."[55] Don't get me wrong on this point. I am not saying that the above named organizations have anything to do with the ungodly history of Nazi Germany. On the contrary, everything they stand for is against such atrocities. But I often sense the same attitudes among some Christians today. When we look to the government to be the protectors of our spiritual values, we may be buying into more than we think.

I don't believe the apostle Paul was defending a particular family form when he encouraged the church to order its family life under the lordship of Christ (Eph. 5–6). Likewise, Paul's political activism seems limited to "submitting to authorities" no matter how ungodly they might be (Rom. 13)[56] and praying for those in power (1 Tim. 2:1–2). He did use his "right of appeal" as a Roman citizen to appeal his unjust arrest to Caesar (Acts 25:10–12), but he did this as a private Roman citizen and not as a Christian. Most Jews in the Roman world did not have this right of appeal!

My personal view is that Christians are most effective when they cannot be confined or tied to partisan politics. I agree with Ed Dobson (not related to James) when he writes, "They [Christian political groups] are selling their religious priorities for a mess of political pottage. In the process, they are harming the gospel. They are implying that there is a proper Christian position on nearly every political issue. They are implying that disagreement with their political positions is, in fact, disagreement with Jesus."[57] Christ has called us to be salt and light to all political parties, even socialistic parties!

During the early 1980s I had the opportunity to teach one summer in Bolivia. At the time, Communist insurgents were active in the countryside. Many of the mountain village churches were pastored by farmers who had fallen under Communist ideology, several of whom were in my class. In my first session these farmers attacked what they thought would be my "American Christian politics." I knew they were influenced by then-popular Marxist Liberation theology, but I did not want to alienate them to such an extent that they would not hear what I was going to teach from Scripture.

I responded by saying, "Look, the only form of government I can find in the Bible is a theocracy, where it was the design to have God rule over the nation of Israel. But throughout Israel's history theocracy was a miserable failure. Second, I can't find any forms of government in the New Testament except the ones that crucified Jesus and imprisoned Paul. So if you want to talk politics we cannot really use Scripture to find an ideal form. We can use it only to argue for principles of justice, benevolence, use of arms, and taxation! The 'Christian forms of government' that these principles have birthed range from the 'Holy Roman Empire' to various monarchies, national parliaments, and republics. As Americans, we obviously think ours is the best!"

My student-pastors finally laughed, expressing the consensus that they could live with my answer and with me. We then jumped into our study of the Gospel of Mark. My view of a particular family model in the Bible is largely the same. Just as I cannot find the concept of a democratic republic divided into three branches of government in the Bible, so I cannot find what is popularly called the "traditional" family. The alert reader might ask at this point, "So what is it about the traditional family model that is unbiblical, impractical, or ambiguous in light of current cultural realities?" To answer the question, I will turn to some of the popular Christian family myths that often appear in biblical guise. Understanding these myths and separating them from simple biblical imperatives will help us see what is distinctively Christian about the family, and what is not.

3

Common Myths about the Christian Family

I hadn't been a Christian long when a fellow believer in my fraternity house took me to a Free Methodist Church. At the time I didn't know a Methodist from a dentist, so I trusted my friend. When we walked into the church I was handed a program, looked down at the order of service, and noticed the sermon topic titled, "The Role of the Husband." Even though I was single at the time I was taken with the message and the pastor's exposition of Ephesians 5 (it took me a long time to find the book of Ephesians). I remember learning for the first time that as a male (when married) I would have the "role" of being the head of my family. At the time, I thought that was kind of "groovy." Today, I'm not so sure. The very concept of "roles" plays into the hand of one of the strongest mythologies about family life.

Myth #1: Marriage Roles Are Determined by Gender

All families *function,* even dysfunctional ones. That is, they get by day to day through some conscious or unconscious method of survival. In family studies literature, families may be evaluated on the basis of roles, rules, or the network of relationships (systems theory). What this first myth underscores is that the way "Christian" marriages are supposed to get by is best accomplished through a role-oriented family structure. Myth #1 basically presupposes an ideal prescribed role for the husband, father, wife, mother, and children. Some researchers have further suggested that within the family structure such things as birth order and personality type become additional roles that get played out within the family. Hence, you have the roles of "first born," the "clown," or the "good girl."[1]

I don't know how many times I've heard the word *role* used in Christian courses on marriage and family. When I am asked, "What is the biblical role for the husband or wife?" my usual response doesn't find much favor with my questioner. I usually reply, "What makes you think there is one?" My questioner commonly responds with something like, "Well, you know that stuff in Ephesians 5." It is amazing how much biblical data can be passed through supposedly attentive listeners without engaging the mind. At this point I ask, "Where do you find the word *role* in Ephesians 5 or in the Bible?" Blank stares usually result. You see, the word *role* never appears in the Bible. So why do we use it? I have no idea.

Webster defines a role as "a socially accepted behavior pattern."[2] What in the world is that? Do I want to run my family by socially accepted behavior patterns?

I have a friend who often reminds me that if the goal of child raising is to make a socially well-adjusted child we are in trouble. He would add, "Those who are well-adjusted to a sick society are sick, not well!" Each word in this phrase is loaded with problems. If our culture deems child molestation "socially acceptable" does that mean it is a fitting thing for parents to do? God forbid! How about the phrase "behavior patterns?" Believing in God, going to church, or not caring for my yard, can all be viewed as behavior patterns to someone. Discerning whether or not they are socially acceptable makes for dangerous territory.

To tell you the truth, I cannot understand why the evangelical community has bought into such an ambiguous term with all its cultural determination. A role is something that society determines and has nothing to do with biblical authority. Therefore, I hesitate to use the term or accept its usage by evangelical writers. There is no role as such for the husband or wife in Scripture. Likewise, there is no role for children, pastors, accountants, or truck drivers!

What the Scriptures *do* teach is a concept of responsibilities. When it comes to family life, biblical material presents its guidance in the grammatical forms of imperatives, prohibitions, and exhortations. What do these imply? Not roles, or sets of rules, but responsibilities. When I ask my son to take out the trash I am not asking him to play a particular role in the family. That is his job. As his father, I am merely telling him the trash needs to be taken out, and I am holding him accountable to do it. No more, no less!

Ask me what the biblical responsibility is for the husband and I can tell you. A husband is to "love his wife as Christ loved the church." It's that simple. But this clear command makes no statement about whether the husband should be the primary wage earner, do dishes, or change diapers. In fact, if he loves his wife as Christ loves the church, it means he will be willing and eager to do any of these. No matter what the cultural stereotypes might be, the husband can do or not do any of the above without violating his responsibility.

Years ago while in the Fiji Islands I had the opportunity to teach on marriage and family issues. My sponsor for the week was a Fijian Ratu, or tribal chief. When I got to teaching on the husband's Christian responsibilities his eyes became large. His wife, sitting next to him, kept giving him the classic elbow nudge to the ribs (a universal sign meaning "I told you so"). At the end of our meeting, the chief got up and confessed to the group how he needed to learn how to change their babies' "nappies." It was quite a stretch for him to come to this position since Fijian tribal society is very traditional with well-defined marital roles, and chiefs don't do diapers! But once he saw that the essential issue was not about roles but the love of Christ and the love of his wife, the conclusion was simple. What was interesting about this experience is that I never once mentioned anything about who should change a baby's diapers. This was what the Spirit of God, and a little nudging from his wife, had apparently laid on the chief's heart. When I left the island they made me an honorary Ratu, one of my most treasured honors.

My concern over the issue of roles is far more than academic semantics. Words impart concepts, and concepts have power; they can encourage and they can harm. It is hard for me to imagine the amount of harm that has been done to Christian husbands, wives, and children in the name of this destructive mythology. Over the years, I have counseled women who struggle with their outgoing "unsubmissive" personalities. They reveal internal struggles of how it seems God cursed them with a kind of personality that just gets them into trouble. When I pastored in one of our eastern states, I met many professional women who were assertive and used to speaking their own minds. Submission, as a role in relation to men in general, didn't fly well with them. One of these women asked me, "Does being a Christian mean that women like us have to turn off our minds and go along with whatever the men in this church want?" Knowing her and the male leaders in the church, I knew she was much more on the ball and had a deeper spirituality than they did. Yet she wondered if God had cursed her with a mind! (In Ephesians wives are asked to submit only to their own husbands, not men in general.)

Likewise, I have known creative men of unique abilities in the arts. These sensitive, sometimes compliant spirits struggle with the "role" of being a leader in the home. Are they less a Christian because they find it difficult to express a John Wayne type of masculinity? Are they less men because of the personality and talents God gave them? When I read the simple statements of Scripture to them, they are set free. Rather than offering a role to play or a set of rules to follow, I let the simple imperative rest with them. I ask, "What does it mean for you to love your wife as Christ does the church?" I allow each individual to figure out what it means in terms of his personal marriage dynamics. Often, the applications men come up with are far more insightful and loving than anything I may conceive.

I have come to understand we do serious harm when we place a concept of roles upon people and ask them to obey a culturally accepted "Christian" set of behaviors. It's far better to do the WWJD thing and ask, How would Jesus love this person? That's my responsibility.

Myth #2: The Husband/Father Is the Head of the Home

Some say it is not only my responsibility to play a particular role, but that my particular function as a male is to be the head of my household, a twin cousin to the first myth. That first sermon I heard on Christian marriage held these two myths as one and the same. They still exist in the evangelical community. With the success of Promise Keepers notwithstanding, I must respond to what I consider a naïve, simplistic, and erroneous view of the family. I do not speak from ignorance, because I served on the Promise Keepers seminar staff; my book *The Masculine Journey* was in their product line, and I spoke at the 1993 national conference in Boulder. The success and value of Promise Keepers is self-evident. It recruited thousands of men to Christ who probably would not have come any other way. However, a mythology about headship seemed to develop as the organization expanded. In mass meetings, men are called upon to come forward and dedicate themselves to going home and being "heads" of their families, sort of taking back the turf they had given over to their wives.

I first saw this mythology in my own church. When men came back from conferences, they told me they needed to take more leadership in their homes. One reporter confirmed this observation: "One speaker challenged men not to 'ask permission for what God commands you to do' as head of the household."[3] When men hear they need to take leadership in the home, mixed with the Ephesians 5 doctrine of headship, many go home to take charge without having a clue as to what it means. A not-so-affirming press noted, "While speakers thundered for a return to a biblically sanctioned 'patriarchal' household and a 'traditional' male order, the rank and file sat quietly."[4] One popular speaker at the conferences, using the language of "Reclaiming Your Manhood," said, "Every man should sit down with his wife and say something like this: 'Honey, I've made a terrible mistake. I've given you my role. I gave up leading this family and I forced you to take my place. Now I must reclaim that role.' . . . I'm not suggesting you ask for your role back, I'm urging you to take it back . . . there can be no compromise here."[5] I still hear such language from men influenced by Promise Keepers. But one publisher wanted to find out what was happening at home after these conferences. A researcher/writer was contracted to do the follow-up work, but unfortunately, the results did not find favor within the organization. Fundamentally, the wives of Promise Keepers were not all that excited about their husband's newfound faith and the implementation of "headship."[6]

It is one thing to tell men to go home and be the head of their homes; it is quite another thing to explain in detail what headship means or does not mean. This element of explanation, in my opinion, was significantly lacking in Promise Keepers meetings and literature. In an interview with author Susan Faludi, even Coach McCartney found it difficult to explain what male leadership should look like. When asked what a spiritual leader is, he replied, "It's my responsibility to encourage others to take some time out, shut off the television, and come before the Lord. See, that's my responsibility to do that. I don't wait for my wife to do it . . . the only way the spiritual work is gonna get done is if the man takes responsibility."[7] In the absence of clear definitions, men were left to figure out for themselves what the words *head* or *leader* meant. My hunch is that a lot of men went home to "take charge" and put things in order, much to the dismay of their wives and sometimes children. Apparently, without the consultation and cooperation of their wives, these men's efforts were viewed not as bettering the family, but in some cases making it worse. Men were often surprised by their wives' reactions. Sometimes, "the women didn't want their husbands' help in their 'domain.'"[8] Even when headship *is* defined it creates problems, but an undefined doctrine of headship thrown out at mass meetings can be lethal.

In addition to the ambiguous nature of the meaning of headship, a related myth exists within the evangelical community. This one I call the "umbrella deduction." This teaching views the husband by virtue of being male and married as the one who has the responsibility of being the spiritual umbrella for his wife and family. In other words, no matter what happens in the family, Dad is responsible! I don't know where this doctrine originated, but I have bumped into it all over the country. Besides being biased against men under the guise of being biblical, it is destructive to their wives. Superficially, the teaching looks appealing to women; after all, it gets them completely off the hook! For men who want to exercise their authority it is a blank check. But in practice, the doctrine is not uniformly applied. As one man said, "I get to be in charge when something goes wrong or we need money." This teaching is not only an unfair doctrine, but, I believe, it is unbiblical. All adult Christians are held equally accountable for their behaviors and responses.

I believe each human being will stand before God and give an account of his or her own life and sins, not someone else's (Rev. 20:12; 1 Cor. 4:5). Besides, when fathers fail to live godly lives before their children, the children are not held accountable for their father's sins. Likewise, when children follow after other gods, the father is not held accountable for his child's sin. Even though a father's sins are "visited" or have an impact upon the next generation (Exod. 20:5), this principle is clear: "The righteousness of the righteous man will be credited to him, and the wickedness of the wicked will be charged against him" (see Ezek. 18:14–20). This is a message rarely taught today. The Lord will certainly ask me if I loved my wife and responsibly cared for my children. But I do not believe the Lord holds me accountable for my wife's failures or my children's sins. We will each stand alone at the judgment seat of Christ, "for we must all appear before the judgment seat of Christ, so that *each one* may be recompensed for his deeds in the body, according to what he has done, whether good or bad" (2 Cor. 5:10 NASB).

Because I am not the Lord's umbrella over my family (only God is our rock and refuge, Ps. 62:7), this does not mean I do not seek to guard their safety or that I ignore their provision. As a responsible Christian man, I must look to the economic provision of my family and all those in need (1 Tim. 3:5; 5:8–10). Scripture does not offer insight into how this provision is to be obtained. It doesn't say who should be earning how much, or who should be paying the bills. The simple point the apostle urges is that the family unit (and others in need) be taken care of, not whether it is achieved through single, double, or multiple family members working. The point lies in being responsible to meet needs, not in *who* does *what.*

Because there is so much confusion about what headship means, let me see if I can add to it with some of my own observations. First, the Greek word for *head* in the New Testament is not all that clear. *Kephale* can denote either a literal physical head or several other metaphorical options. Metaphorical meanings of *kephale* include "superior rank, the keystone or capstone over a door; a cornerstone, or the uppermost part of something."[9] Debate rages over whether or not the idea of authority is resident in the term. One writer prefers the idea of headship as "the fountainhead of life."[10]

Whatever the term means in places like Ephesians 5, a couple of things *are* clear: It is wrong to assume that a word in one language means the same thing in another language. It is equally just as wrong to assume that each time a word like *kephale* appears in the New Testament, it means the same thing. Furthermore, no matter what the word *head* means in the passage, it is the responsibility of the *head* to love sacrificially. Husbands are to love their own wives as Christ loved the church and gave himself for her. Even if the idea of authority exists in headship, the passage still means the same thing: husbands, as authoritative heads, are to love by sacrificing. Frankly, I can't understand why there is so much confusion about the responsibility of the husband. It seems everyone gets hung up on the authority issue and misses the whole point of the passage.

To add one more thought to the confusion, even if the husband has authority, so does the wife. The apostle Paul uses the common Greek word for authority *(exousia)* in

1 Corinthians 7:4 to demonstrate that both the husband and wife have authority over each other. Here, the meaning of *exousia* is clear; it means "bearer of authority as in one of official power."[11] Though the specific context has to do with a couple's sexual relationship, I would grant the principle can and should be applied to other areas as well. In other words, authority is shared in the husband/wife relationship and is not the sole responsibility or "role" of one or the other.

A passage that rarely appears in this debate is 1 Timothy 5:14, where Paul encourages younger widows to marry, have children, and as my translation says, "keep house." Here, Paul uses one of the strongest terms for authority in all of Greek literature: *despotes.* Combined with the word for house, *oikos,* we have the verb *oikodespotein.* A literal rendering of the term would be "master or lord of the house."[12] In other words, Paul is affirming the common acknowledgment at the time of writing that wives "rule" the home. They are the house-despots! They exercise authority in the home, and maybe even more authority than their husbands. Isn't this the issue that Promise Keepers' wives were complaining about? Their husbands came home and tried to take over their domain! The wives' response was, "Thank you very much, but I've been managing just fine."

What all this goes to show is how naïve and biblically uninformed are those who argue the simple claim that the husband is the head of the home. In fact, those exact words are never found in the text. The husband is said to be the head of his *wife,* not the *home.* If anything, both realistically and biblically, it is the wife who is the head or master of the home. My personal view is that both have authority in the home and each must be willing to give up that authority in order to achieve mutual submission and love. The husband's responsibility is focused on the relational and communicational aspects of his wife (head and body metaphor) while exercising general oversight of the household along with her (one of the elder qualifications listed in 1 Tim. 3:4).[13] I have found that the wives effectively manage and direct domestic concerns even when working full-time outside the home. In fact, they still feel responsible and take responsibility for the house and all its functions even when the husband is at home doing domestic chores.

In short, I contend that the ideal of husband as the singular head of the home is a myth. It is not valid in principle except where the male is a single father. Further, this is an impossible role to pull off consistently. In fact, in a biblical theology this role is just a master-servant paradigm rooted in a parent-child relationship, where obedience to authority is the goal (closer to the Ephesians 6:1 relation of parent and child). This is a far cry from the loving relationship of mutual submission clearly taught in Ephesians 5. As noted, the word *head* is biblically ambiguous. If the singular meaning of "authority" is embraced in extreme cases, the totalitarian "headship" of the husband can become highly abusive. One study indicated that "a strong belief in the man's power within his family without some surveillance or checks" can easily lead to child or spouse abuse, and incest.[14] Mythologies may fill in the gaps where sufficient education is lacking, but the reality is that family mythologies can become destructive.

Myth #3: Family Health and Happiness Is Obtained by Fulfilling a Particular Role

I don't know how many times I've listened to evangelical authorities on the subject of the family reduce complex family functioning to the big three: (1) Getting the children of all ages to obey; (2) wives being submissive to their husbands; (3) husbands being the heads of the households. On the macro scale, simplistic answers also abound. If couples would just stay together, if mothers just stayed at home, or if men would really be men, then the family crisis could be averted. All these statements reflect the notion that family living in modern times has changed. Indeed, changes have come, but I don't believe these changes necessarily reflect a crisis or need to result in one. I may not like change, and change usually creates a crisis within me, but my individual crisis does not mean there is a much larger family crisis going on. If a gay couple moves into my neighborhood, it doesn't imply the American family is falling apart.

Trying to figure out what it is that creates family health and happiness is about as difficult as nailing Jell-O to the wall. My Reformed friends would say health and happiness lie in obedience to God. I believe this is true if we define happiness as blessedness. But unfortunately, most don't. When we think of family happiness most think of fuzzy, close feelings. But does pure obedience result in these feelings? The myth lies in thinking that if we each perform our role well (being obedient to what we think is biblical), then happiness will result painted in Norman Rockwell hues. Children (including adolescents) will be well-behaved, be polite, and show respect to their siblings and elders. They will appear to be good, especially at church, never create disruptions or challenge authority, and look adoringly clean-cut in their matching polo shirts. In this scenario, children's health is seen as passivity, with the absence of behavioral problems.

Mutuality, affection, and the absence of conflict characterize the husband-wife relationship in this mythology. When I pastored a church in Hawaii we had several Japanese-American families in our fellowship. I found it difficult to teach on Christian marriage while being confronted with the fact that so many assumptions about how to love are purely American. In Japanese culture many American expressions of marital love are viewed as public impropriety, nothing more than fixations on sexuality. To the Japanese, a man holding his wife's hand or kissing his wife in public is pure Americanism. To Americans, love easily gets translated as kissing or hand holding. I surely enjoy kissing my wife, but is this act uniquely Christian? No. Though the Bible does record acts of kissing (Song of Songs 1:2; Gen. 29:11), one recorded public display of affection is when Isaac fondles Rebekah and it gets him into trouble with the Philistine king (Gen. 26:8).

In the myth of role playing, the husband-wife relationship encounters no serious struggles, competing values, ideas, or careers. Marital health is proved by the absence of problems and implies the couple's agreement on most issues. The underlying assumption is that women should find their fulfillment (happiness) in raising children and submitting to their husbands. Likewise, the husband should find his fulfillment in working hard, earning a good living, and leading the family.

Why is it that so many couples have done these things and not found the joy and happiness they thought was promised? Worse, some Christian couples begin to view their marriage as a giant commercial for God. In public, they play as if they are happy and fulfilled in order to show outsiders how good God is. In reality, their family life and marriage may be a sham; most commercials lie! I don't know how many times I have heard about the "perfect couple" quietly disappearing from church, and then learned they have divorced. Did they not have the freedom to share their difficulties or would that have blown the whistle on their commercial marriage?

What is amazing about my work with men over the years is how few are really happy and fulfilled in their work. Yes, they work hard and encounter significant loss when out of work, but for most of them work is something they tolerate. It is a matter of survival necessary to support a family. When honest, most men reveal they find their fulfillment and joy in other things, usually their families, sports, hobbies, or avocations. Men who enjoy their work usually have found ways to combine their avocations with their vocation, or they are compulsive workaholics who just love being busy.

Women, likewise, face similar frustrations. I've known Christian women who confess during counseling they find more fulfillment in their career than in mothering. This is not to say they are bad or irresponsible mothers. In most cases, I thought they were great mothers, but how they evaluated their inner spirits was far different from how people on the outside saw them.

It is legitimate to ask, Where should both husbands and wives find fulfillment and happiness? There is certainly nothing wrong in finding happiness in family life, but is the institution of marriage and the bearing of children supposed to be the source of adult health? If it is, that places an extreme pressure upon the family while excluding never-married adults from happiness. Most married couples begin with this assumption: "I will marry this person because he/she will make me happy." But what happens when the person is no longer the source or the object of one's happiness? I believe we have looked in the wrong place for happiness and asked our mates, even our children, to give us what only God can give. And sometimes, it seems even he lets us down.

Our supreme joy should be found in God, of course, but much of life is not joyous. Yes, marriage and family life bring considerable joy, but they also carry pain, sorrow, and heartbreak. If you hold the expectation that perpetual happiness is dependent upon fallible human beings, then I wish you lots of luck! What keeps me in the faith is knowing I have an infallible God who will use everything in my life for his glory. This belief does not take away the pain, sorrow, or struggle I often feel.

I do not seek fulfillment in playing a particular role; remember, I don't believe in roles anyway. I don't look to my mate, my marriage, or my kids to make me happy. Happiness is too complex a thing for any one human being to bring about in another person for very long. When I meet my biblical responsibilities I should not seek to be blessed with happiness as if it were part of some divine contract; like, "I'll do your will, and in return you make me be happy." I don't think God delights in these little psychological contracts we formulate. The only contract God has made with us is the new covenant in Jesus' blood. This covenant has nothing to do with my happiness, only my holiness in Christ, and the assurance of having my sins forgiven. This should make me happy and often does, but there are still areas of my life where miserable feelings are present.

We must seek to meet our biblical responsibilities not because they bring us happiness, but because they are the right and proper things to do. It is in our interest before God to do them because God cares for us and has not left us without direction in this chaotic world. Following his guidance may not necessarily make me happier, but it gets me where I need to go. On the other hand, if I chose to go my own way and end up wandering around, unhappiness is sure to follow. In family life, we should desire to fulfill our biblical responsibilities without expecting some specific return on our obedience. We should find a deep sense of joy in knowing what we have done is right and good before God, no matter what the results.

Myth #4: Parents Are the Primary Determiners of a Child's Success

I once heard the popular writer and speaker Tony Campolo address a Sunday school class. He began the hour by throwing out the question, "Why have kids?" The predictable evangelical responses came back: "They are a blessing from God." "God commands us to be fruitful, and they will bear witness to our faith." In characteristic fashion, Tony Campolo played off every response. He reminded the audience of the cost of having children today and how they are no longer economic producers, but, in fact, economic liabilities. There used to be a time when children, especially sons, were needed to ensure that family property and money would stay in the family name (laws of primogeniture). This argument no longer holds water. Now property can be willed to anyone, and who cares if money stays in the family? Finally, the class gave up and someone asked, "Then why are we still having kids"?

Campolo laughed and said, "There is only one reason left."

Everyone was baited and ready for the final answer. Campolo shocked us by saying, "For what they can do for us!"

What he was implying is that in a technological and materialistic society, the only reason left to have children is as a symbol of a parent's identity and success. Children become proof of how good a parent we are, a symbol of our achievements. In other words, children are needed to validate the parent's status, identity, and goals.

In a society that has moved from extended families to nuclear families, the only ones left to either be praised or blamed is the parents. When children are not doing well at school, educators blame the parents while parents blame the teachers. The ludicrous circle of blame illustrates the mythology that parents are all-powerful, having total control over their children's lives. The myth makes parents the only determiners of a child's success, whatever that means. It also makes them totally responsible for the child's failure. This is unfair, unrealistic, and anything but biblical.

A major contributor to this myth is the at-risk industry. Yes, I call it an industry because a network of educators, psychologists, and publishers exists and benefits by promoting parents as the sole determiners of a child's success. This industry affirms the role-playing mythology through the back door of the children at-risk ideology. Coontz observes the following:

> If you stayed too long in the Jacuzzi or took a couple of drinks during pregnancy, your baby is "at risk" for learning disabilities. If you failed to bond with your infant in the critical early months or even minutes, your child is "at risk" for insecure attachment. If you put your boy in a certain kind of day care at a particular age, he is "at risk"; if you don't put your girl in the same kind of day care at the same age, she is "at risk". If you are divorced, your kids are "at risk". If you and your spouse stayed together for the sake of the kids and couldn't hide the tension, then they are still "at risk". And if your own behavior hasn't put your kids at risk, their future is threatened by the parents who have ruined their kids, causing the rise in crime and the disintegration of our schools.
>
> To some extent, of course, all our children are "at risk", because we are fallible human beings in a society that expects us single-handedly, or at most two-parently, to counter all the economic ups and downs, social pressures, personal choices, and competing demands of a highly unequal, consumption-oriented culture dominated by deteriorating working conditions, interest-group politics, and self-serving advertisements for everything from toothpaste to moral values.
>
> As a historian, I suspect that the truly dysfunctional thing about American parenting is that it is made out to be such a frighteningly pivotal, private and exclusive job.[15]

One popular writer has gone so far as to say that 96 percent of the American population has come from dysfunctional families.[16] I don't believe this statistic for the simple reason that it is difficult to prove. It also implies that 100 percent of the population has either taken a survey or been in some kind of therapy with an official diagnosis. Both are impossible to prove. But statistics like this breed the at-risk mind-set, which in turn makes parent the sole determiner of childhood health or sickness.

This myth creates the assumption that parents have the critical control over how their children turn out. Child developmentalist Judith Harris says, "Parenting has been oversold. You have been led to believe that you have more of an influence in your child's personality than you really do."[17]

In reality, a number of factors determine a child's success or failure, none having anything to do with the family. Teachers, coaches, and friends played significant roles in making me who I am. Being a child of the first television generation played, in addition, an extremely powerful role in my upbringing. John Wayne, Roy Rogers, and Gene Autry were the males who became my heroes. What I learned from playing sports and my struggle with trumpet lessons were all influences on my life. Seeing an American president assassinated and witnessing how a society tried to deal with it were a slice of the life curriculum I experienced. Also, dating the same girl through junior and senior high schools established many of my values about dating, relationships, and sexuality.

Harris illuminates the issue this way:

> Our childhood experiences with peers and our experiences at home with our parents are important to us in different ways. The bond between parent and child lasts a lifetime. We kiss our parents goodbye not once but many times; we do not lose track of them. Each visit home gives us opportunities to take our family memories and look at them again. Meanwhile, our childhood friends have scattered to the winds and we've forgotten what happened on the playground. When you think about childhood you think

> about your parents. Blame it on the relationship department of your mind, which has usurped more than its rightful share of your thoughts and memories. As for what's wrong with you: don't blame it on your parents.[18]

"The myth of the vulnerable child exaggerates both the power of the parent and the passivity of the child," writes research psychologist Arlene Skolnick. "In fact, parents seldom have 'make or break' control over the child's growth,"[19] she says.

Apart from the general New Testament admonition for fathers to raise their children in the nurture and admonition of Christ (Eph. 6:4), one must go to the Book of Proverbs to find detailed insight about parenting. First, there is a straightforward acknowledgment of what parents feel about their children: "A foolish son is a grief to his father and bitterness to her who bore him" (Prov. 17:25 RSV). Notice this does not say the son is a fool because of something his father or mother did, or did not do, something the at-risk industry would conclude. The proverb merely asserts the reality that parents bear the grief of their children's failures and pain. Here, it is the parents who bear shame for the child's wrong behavior, not the other way around. In a second proverb we find, "The father of the righteous will greatly rejoice; he who begets a wise son will be glad in him" (23:24–25 RSV). Here, the writer merely records the reality of joyous parental feelings. When parents see wisdom and righteousness in a child, they rejoice. That's the common, ordinary reaction. Again, there is no statement that the child's righteousness is any way connected to the parents.

What the parent/child proverbs demonstrate is that parents can encourage their children by example and exhortation. Solomon says a man "directed and led his son in upright paths," not dragged him in a direction he did not want to go (see Prov. 4:11). Likewise, he asks his son to "listen to his instruction, and not forsake the teaching of his mother" (see 1:8–9; 6:20–23).

Throughout this literature there is an assumption about the nature of the child. The assumption is that he or she will have the tendency to stray, enticed by a whole range of foolish behaviors. What is strangely missing is any connection to the parent. Sister Wisdom in Proverbs is a realist. In one of the opening chapters, she announces, "My son, *if* you accept my words . . . and cry aloud for understanding, . . . *if* you look for it [wisdom] as for silver, . . . then you will understand the fear of the Lord and find the knowledge of God" (Prov. 2:1–6, italics added). The if-then clauses make this entire process conditional. There is nothing assured here. It also places the behavioral responsibility firmly upon the child, not the parent.

It is up to the child eventually to decide for himself how he wants to live, whom he wants to listen to, and what path his life should take.[20] Scripture doesn't play games with us. Raising offspring is presented as a dynamic, ever changing interaction between parent and child in which nothing is fixed or promised. Parents are held accountable for their example and exhortation only, while the child bears the responsibility for his own actions. Parents share in the joy of their children's success while bearing the shame of their children's failures. I agree with Clapp's conclusion: "For all our scientific understanding, for all our child psychology, children—even modern children—remain mysterious."[21]

Myth #5: The Christian Family Is Defined by Biologically or Legally Related People Living in the Same Domicile

During the administration of President Jimmy Carter, the first White House Conference on the Family was held. At least that's the way the original announcement was made. By the time the conference was held the title had become the White House Conference on Families, because once the original title was released every gay rights group came out of the woodwork protesting that they were families too. With the inability of the planners to come up with an exact definition of what constituted a family, they opted for the pluralistic term "families." Unfortunately, evangelicals reacted to the liberalizing tendency of the administration without thinking about how we might approach a broader concept of family. Most Christians assume that family means either a biological or legal relationship. In other words, for a family to be Christian, it must be related by blood or legal arrangement (marriage or adoption). This is a limited view of family and one that is far from the teaching of Scripture.

Scripture recognizes the importance of the biological family in the founding of the nation of Israel and the family of Abraham (Gen. 12:1–3). But it also recognizes nonblood relationships when derived through marriage as in the case of Ruth and Naomi (Ruth 1:4) and nonlegal relationships. The major obstacle in understanding this lies in the fact that there is no equivalent word for family in either the Old or New Testament. The Hebrew word usually translated "family" is *mishpat*. However, contextual usage offers a variety of meanings for this: "clan," "nation," or "guilds." The related term, *shephchah*, can be translated as "maidservant," "menial-house servants," or "concubine."[22] When the Greek Old Testament was translated from Hebrew, the term used to translate *mishphat* was *phule*, meaning "a body of people united by kinship or habitation."[23] In other words, a family is anyone living in the same house.

One writer notes, "The organization of the tribal life of the Hebrews is based on the primary cell of the family with the father as head. The union of several families (1 Chron. 23:11) forms the 'house' of the father."[24] This sheds light on Jesus' teaching about the house of his father (John 14:1–2). Jesus has gone to prepare a place for us; a group of nonblood, nonlegal followers who will occupy the house of his father as family! The same idea sheds light on Paul's teaching about being in the household of faith and a member of God's household (Eph. 2:19; 1 Tim. 3:15). The theology is clear: We become a member of God's family by taking up residence under his roof. It is Christ who invites us to his father's house and grants us entry through his blood (Matt. 11:28; 1 Peter 2:5).

I am not naturally given to hospitality, but in over thirty years of marriage, God has blessed our home with several nonrelated people who became family to us. We took in a young single woman who had no one to care for her after a surgery, and a male friend diagnosed with multiple sclerosis who had lost his marriage and his job and found himself without adequate medical care or lodging. Our kids sat on Dennis's lap and pushed him around in his wheelchair. We celebrated Christmas and attended church together. Other "family members" have come and gone. One slept on our couch, ate our food, and did odd jobs around our house before he found another place to stay. A seminary student lived with us for a couple of terms. Between classes, dating, and working at a restaurant, he would sit at our kitchen table eating restaurant leftovers and talking theology. Being under our roof made these people family. Maybe the biblical definition of family as people united by kinship or habitation is more accurate and workable than what is commonly thought of as the traditional family.

Another aspect to the myth of the ideal family is that some in the traditional camp make family the most important institution on earth. Therefore, it appeals to politicians who support it in order to get votes. But may I raise a question about this? Don't get me wrong; I believe the family is vitally important to the health of any society. But throughout the centuries, the family has changed its structure, adjusted to new demands and crises, and survived. What this suggests is that the "Christian-ness" of the family does not lie in its form, but elsewhere. Where might that be?

I am often asked if I am a dispensationalist since I went to Dallas Theological Seminary and was on the faculty there. My standard response is, "Yes, but I hold to some different dispensations than the ones I was taught." One of them is found in Mark 3:31–35.[25] Most know the story well, but the implications are rarely applied to the doctrine of the family. Jesus was teaching a cross-section of people packed into a room while his mother and brothers were outside the house in which he was teaching. Get the picture? Here was a collection of "hoi polloi," literal for "multitude." This was apparently a random collection of nonrelated people sitting around the feet of their house patriarch, Jesus. When told that his mother and brothers were calling for him outside, Jesus' answer seems surprisingly cold. Remember previous to this event, his biological family thought he had absolutely lost his senses (Mark 3:21). Now he replies with a question that makes a significant dispensational shift in the economy of God. He asks, "Who are my mother and my brothers?" Apparently there was no answer, so after a pause Jesus looks directly at those gathered in the room and proclaims, "Here are my mother and brothers! Whoever does God's will is my brother and sister and mother."

What has taken place here? In the Old Testament, the family form was for the most part patriarchal based on blood relations and kinship. Even servants and concubines who lived in the same house were afforded family status. But here, there is a shift rarely mentioned in theological circles. Jesus has in one sense rejected the traditional definition of family as a biological or marital relation. In the New Testament, family will be defined as "those who do

God's will." The distinctive Christian element of family has nothing to do with bloodlines or marital relationships. It has more to do with the spiritual commitment of the individual. The new household of faith consists of those who sit at the feet of Jesus and are commited to doing his will. As will be addressed later, the Epistles do address fathers, mothers, and children as members of households, but the primary emphasis on the subject of family is the spiritual family relations we have in Christ—not our earthly biological families (Eph. 2:19; 1 Peter 2:5). This means we need to broaden our concept of Christian family to one that includes single mothers, single adults, foster children, orphans, strangers, and anyone who is willing to sit at the feet of Jesus. It also means broadening our concept of family to anyone showing up on our doorstep in need.

The impact of this is significant; could it be the myth of the ideal has made the biological family a higher priority than what is biblical? Family relations are important and need to be regulated by biblical responsibilities, but they are not all-important. We must always bear in mind that Jesus himself cautioned that our greatest enemy will come from within our own home. In addition, Christ carried out his entire ministry while a single adult and living as an exile from his biological family (Matt. 10:32–39). Paul likewise encouraged singleness for the kingdom of God and played down the benefits of marriage (1 Cor. 7:32–35). Clapp says: "The family is not God's most important institution on earth. The family is not the social agent that most significantly shapes and forms the character of Christians. The family is not the primary vehicle of God's grace and salvation for a waiting, desperate world . . . we cannot put Jesus first and still put family first."[26]

Few realize how myths undermine family health. Myths cause us to distort or devalue our unique family experience because they are viewed through a faulty lens, a lens of what ought to be but cannot be. They create unrealistic expectations that in turn make us think there is something wrong with us. We ask why our family is not doing as well as someone else's family. In the final analysis, myths are rooted in good ol' American middle-class stuff and a perceived Christian consensus about what Scripture teaches rather than Scripture itself. Myths function in such a way as to make us think, *This is the way it ought to be.* But we need to understand the "traditional" family is neither the way it ought to be, nor has it ever been.

I've tried to dispel assumptions about how Christian families operate or understand themselves. My intent is to demythologize mistaken notions. In the next section, I want to construct a different approach to family life. This one will move us from thinking about particular family roles, rules, and structures into a biblical theology of family life. Then we'll draw some conclusions about what the Bible suggests in terms of living a Christian life in postmodern culture.

4

What Biblical Families Look Like in the Old Testament

When I teach on the subjects covered in the previous chapters, my audience usually becomes pretty frustrated. Having looked at the various media myths and then dispelling some of the common Christian myths, someone will ask, "So what is the biblical model of family life?" Equating the traditional model with the biblical model they assume the teaching must be in there somewhere. What I want to demonstrate in this chapter is that Scripture does not give us any one model of family life. What is found is a repeated emphasis on certain family dynamics, functions, and ethics. When taken together, these give us an excellent approach to family life.

How Theologies Are Constructed

Simply defined, theology is the study of God. A fuller definition sheds light on the fact that theologies do not magically appear out of heaven. They are written by men (and now women) and have to do with the process of obtaining data from Scripture and other sources and arranging it into a coherent package. The final form or arrangement reveals many contributors, the individual presuppositions of the collector, current theological, philosophical, and cultural issues, and the amount of data to be included. Obviously no theology can cover every verse of Scripture or every aspect of a subject. Therefore some data has to be excluded. Theologies, then, reflect the limitations of the individual theologian, his own time and place in history, and data available to him. As evangelicals, we believe God has revealed himself in Scripture, but the process of interpreting this revelation and formulating it into a theology is a very human process. This is an important distinction to be observed because we do not want to equate revelation with the spurious opinions of men. Theological discussion (including mine) is merely a reflection and interpretation of biblical data.

"Theology is and always has been a human work," Gordon Kaufman writes. "It is founded upon and interprets human historical events and experiences; it utilizes humanly created and shaped terms and concepts; it is carried out by human processes of meditation, reflection, speaking, writing and reading."[1]

When looking at historical narrative sections of Scripture, I assume the portraits found there are telling us what families did and how they lived without making any statement about how they ought to live. How biblical characters lived in terms of family organization or roles may have been the same as pagan families of the era. After all, most families in the ancient world were a patriarchal organization with the husband as head. The fact that patriarchal families are found in Israel is not unique. The unique element of Hebrew families lies not in their organization but their belief in the one true God, Yahweh. Therefore, to determine the moral and ethical issues related to family life, we must study specific biblical imperatives, exhortations, and prohibitions. As noted earlier, grammatically commands and exhortations (from a superior to an inferior as in God to man) focus on responsibilities. These responsibilities illustrate how God desires families to live without making any statement about their form.

Is There a Biblical Ideal?

Let's suppose there is a biblical model of the family. Where would we find it?

Apparently, Adam and Eve had a great relationship until sin entered and their idyllic relationship changed forever. Deceit, blame, and irresponsibility began eroding their relationship. They tried to hide their sin and hide from God. Once children were born, spiritual jealousy bred hostile feelings that in turn led to the first murder, where Cain killed his brother, Abel (Gen. 4:1–15). This first family is not exactly a sterling example; no one wants to claim them as the biblical model.

When the legacy of the first family became abhorrent, God determined to do away with his creation of mankind (Gen. 6:5–7). Fortunately, one family "found favor in the eyes of the LORD," the family of Noah. Although Noah was a "righteous man, blameless . . . in his time," after the flood he got drunk and his son Ham looked upon his nakedness. The action brings judgment on the entire lineage of Ham (Gen. 9:19–25).[2] In light of this example, would anyone want to claim Noah's family as the biblical ideal?

Perhaps we can do better with Abraham, the patriarch of the Hebrew nation. Certainly here is a man who trusts in the Lord, erects memorials of faith, and calls on the name of the Lord. But he is also a polygamist and a liar and easily manipulated by his wife. When Sarah wants a child without waiting on God's timing and intervention, Abraham gives in to her desire to produce a child by Hagar, Sarah's tent maiden (Gen. 16).

Abraham's children are not any better. The father's habit of telling half-truths is expanded to outright deceitful relations in the life of his grandson, Jacob. Abraham's daughter-in-law Rebekah is the instigator of a deceitful theft resulting in blessing being placed on Jacob rather than his brother, Esau. Jacob's family becomes a classic study of dysfunction. Deceit, jealousy, rape, and attempted murder are all found in the sons of Jacob. Only Joseph appears as an example of grace during the period; at least he forgives his brothers for selling him into slavery and views it as God's providential plan (Gen. 50:20). So if we want a biblical model of family life, I don't think we want to emulate the family dynamics of father Abraham or his offspring.

When we think of godly living in the Old Testament, King David comes to mind. He wrote many of the psalms and is called "a man after God's own heart." But what about David's family life? In spite of what we learn about David in the psalms, the biblical narratives do not paint David in the same light. In many ways, he is far more spiritually minded before he becomes king. Once in power, his family relationships deteriorate. David, like Abraham, was a polygamist with eight wives, most notably Bathsheba, the wife he stole from one of his faithful soldiers. Being responsible for her husband's murder, he takes Bathsheba as his own wife. After this, David's relationship with his son Absalom is so bad it leads to a revolt. Having accomplished the coup, Absalom humiliates his father in public by having sexual relations with all of David's concubines on the roof of the palace.

After being restored to his throne, David desires to build a house for the Lord. God, however, forbids it, saying David has too much blood on his hands. David's attempt to number the size of his army results in a serious plague that claims 70,000 lives (2 Sam. 24. God apparently does not want David trusting in his military capability!). On his deathbed, David gives his son Solomon a hit list to carry out against all those who offended him during his lifetime. In his final moments, the only comfort he obtains is from a beautiful girl (1 Kings 1:4), a strange way for a great and godly man to die. So what kind of family does the life of David illustrate? Certainly not a model we would want to emulate.

Solomon, David's heir to the throne, is not much better. True, he loved the Lord, but he also loved wealth and especially women (1 Kings 11:4). It is recorded he did everything God forbid kings to do (Deut. 17:14–20). He multiplied horses, gold, silver, and women; he had seven hundred wives and three hundred concubines (Eccles. 2:8; 1 Kings 11:3)! After Solomon's reign, the kingdom of Israel split in two, proving that a divided man leaves the legacy of a divided kingdom. The remainder of the monarchy period is not better. There are a few good kings here and there, but for the most part family models go downhill.

The job description of Israel's prophets centered on their condemnation of the nation's sins. God asked the prophet Hosea to marry a harlot as an illustration of how Israel had married itself to a spirit of harlotry (Hosea 1:2; 4:10–14). The prophet Ezekiel confirmed that Israel's unfaithfulness in family life was illustrative of their unfaithfulness to the Lord (Ezek. 16). The Old Testament ends with the prophet Malachi yearning for and looking forward to the promised time when Elijah will return and restore the hearts of fathers to their children, and children to their fathers (Mal. 4:5–6). Thus, it is hard to find a fitting model of family life during the prophetic period, and the ones we do find are severely flawed.

How Shall We Then Live?

If an ideal or prescribed model of family life cannot be found in the Old Testament, how can we best approach the subject of family life? Let's cover the same territory but with a different set of eyes. Instead of trying to find a model in terms of clear structure, let's look at assumptions about family life highlighted by clear commands and exhortations, centering on the role of function rather than form.

Pre-Patriarchal Family Dynamic

Priority of Husband-Wife Relationship

In the early chapters of the Bible, the pre-patriarchal period affirms the priority of the husband-and-wife relationship (Gen. 2:24). The climax of God's creative handiwork is seen in the establishment of a man and woman living together in all their creational gender differences. Centuries later when Jesus is confronted about the issue of divorce, he will argue back to this original divine design for marriage (Matt. 19:5).

Raising Spiritually Minded Children

A second important teaching that emerges is the significance of children. From Adam to Noah, both the destructive capability of children (Gen. 4:8, 19) and the reproductive responsibility of parents (1:28; 9:1, 19) are observed. As family genealogies are traced, one can easily see the importance of raising a spiritually minded progeny over against more earthly concerns of empire building and becoming technocrats: The line of Seth builds a family lineage characterized by long life, while the line of Cain builds cities and masters technology (Gen. 4:16–25; 5:6–32).

Family Accountability

With the reality and responsibility of children comes the concept of family accountability. Adam is held accountable for the actions of his wife, and Cain is held accountable for the life of his brother Abel. In Noah's time, God makes it clear that all men are accountable for their fellow man. Hence, taking another human life reveals the ultimate failure of this virtue; the offender must sacrifice his own life for the blood that was shed (Gen. 9:6).

From the family of Noah we learn his sons were accountable for their behavior in regard to their intoxicated father. Shem and Japheth are commended for covering up their father, thus showing respect for him, while Ham fails in this responsibility and suffers a curse on his children (9:25). From the viewpoint of these passages it seems clear that family accountability and an expected solidarity of family commitment is expected.

Personal Relationship with God

It is also noteworthy to observe that during this early pre-patriarchal age there existed a personal Godward relationship about family life. The noticeable lack of this relationship is seen in the line of Cain. After the death of Abel, Eve conceives again and gives birth to Seth, who is the favored divine replacement. It was at this point that men began to call upon the name of Lord (Gen. 4:1, 26); later Noah walked with God (6:9), building an altar to Yahweh (8:20).

Patriarchal Family Dynamic

During the patriarchal period a family became a nation. From Abraham's seed an entire nation of families was created. In spite of family decline, the institution of family survived and the reader can learn much about family functioning. The contrast from earlier chapters of Genesis is significant. John Davis notes:

> The line of Abraham is characterized more by tents and altars. The first eleven chapters of Genesis possess a uni-

versal and cosmic emphasis, but with the introduction of Abraham, Moses, under the inspiration of the Holy Spirit, begins to particularize redemptive history. God's covenant with Abraham, like a thin thread drawn taut, often appears about to be snapped by the impropriety of Abraham or the pressures of the people around him. It is at this very point of tension that we are able to view most clearly the spectacle of divine providence.[3]

Parental Blessing

Of great importance in the Old Testament is the bestowing of personal blessing by a father upon his children. Both the withholding and granting of parental blessing demonstrate profound developmental power. When the blessing is withheld (a symbol of rejection), severe jealousy, conflict, and outright hatred is observed in family dynamics. Gary Smalley and John Trent comment:

> When Esau lost his blessing from his father, he was devastated. In fact, when he discovered that Jacob had stolen the blessing, Esau cried out, "Do you have only one blessing, my father? Bless me, even me also, O my father!" (Gen. 27:38). For a father in biblical times, once a blessing was spoken, it was irretrievable. In response to his pitiful cries, Esau did receive a blessing of sorts from his father (Gen. 27:39–40), but it was not the words of value and acceptance that he had longed to hear. Can you feel the anguish in the cry, "Bless me, even me also, O my father"? This painful cry and unfulfilled longing is being echoed today by many people who are searching for their family's blessing, men and women whose parents, for whatever reason, have failed to bless them with words of love and acceptance.[4]

Family Unity and Solidarity

Family unity and solidarity is observed when Abraham rescues his nephew Lot and young Joseph protects and provides for his own brothers who sold him into slavery.

The protective solidarity is extended to all family members, including in-laws. The historical narrative continues to underscore the fact that we are our brother's keeper (Gen. 4:9), in opposition to the example of Cain. The lack of this trait is particularly noticeable in the family dynamics of Isaac and Jacob, Joseph being the exception.

Sexual Fidelity

Another characteristic of family functioning during the patriarchal period is the apparent normality of sexual expression. In the marriages of Abraham and of Isaac, the husband-wife sexual relationship is presented as a pleasurable experience (Gen. 18:12). The fondling of a wife's breasts (26:8) and an understanding of sexual reproduction in the coitus interruptus of Onan (38:9) are recorded without ethical comment. But sexual fidelity is emphasized indirectly through the negative results produced from illicit sexual activity, jealousy between Sarah and Hagar, and ongoing examples of the use of concubines, prostitution, and rape where warfare, death, and dysfunction are consequences.

Family as a System

"Family System" theory is fairly recent, but much can be seen through the relationship between marital dynamics and parenting skills in the Bible. In the families of Isaac and of Jacob, conflict and the absence of togetherness in the husband-wife relationship can be viewed as causal and preparatory to sibling conflict. Isaac prays that barren Rebekah will have children, but when she finally gives birth to twins, Esau and Jacob, the result is sibling rivalry rooted in Mom and Dad's differing favorites. Rebekah loves Jacob and Isaac loves Esau; thus the power alliances are divided.

Jacob's dysfunctional family can be easily explained by early marital dynamics. His romantic love affair with

Rachel is tarnished by the deception of his own father-in-law, Laban, and results in rival affections between Rachel and her sister Leah. Jacob ends up with two wives while also fathering children by two maidservants (Gen. 30:1–12). Sibling rivalry leads to the hatred and expulsion of Joseph. Joseph's brother Judah marries a Canaanite (38:2–3) while Onan, Judah's son, sexually and maliciously misuses his brother's wife (38:9). This family is a mess because strained marital dynamics lead to dysfunctional relations in successive generations.

Need for Divine Intervention

Allowed to continue without some divine confrontation, Abraham, Isaac, and Jacob would not have responded to God. In grace, God becomes the family interventionist. He speaks, makes promises, blesses, and even "wrestles" with Jacob in order to bring about divine purposes on earth. This offers hope that Josephs can emerge from the most dysfunctional of families.

Family Dynamic of the Legal Period

The families of Abraham, Isaac, and Jacob are left in Egypt for 430 years. During this time, they grow in numbers, becoming a serious threat to Egyptian power. Moses, who is both Egyptian prince and Hebrew deliverer, has the task of not only delivering the nation by crossing the Red Sea, but also regulating a nation of families. In the wilderness experience, God gives Moses divine laws for social, spiritual, and family health. Much of the material recorded in the books of Exodus, Leviticus, Deuteronomy, and Numbers relates directly to family life. In other words, God himself, the one who birthed the nation, gives his people the guidance they need to live well (Deut. 29:9). From this vast amount of material, eight imperatives can be observed.

Honor God and Life

The first and most obvious legal period imperative implies that honoring of God leads to the honoring of life, property, marriage, and the family unit (Exod. 1:17, 20; 21:22; Lev. 19:3, 32; 25:11; Num. 27:3–11; Deut. 13:6–9; 21:10–14). The Ten Commandments, rooted in a strict monotheism, affirm respect for life in "thou shall not murder." "Thou shall not commit adultery" protects the sanctity of the marriage relationship. "Thou shall not steal" affirms respect for individual property. The conclusion is undeniable: Respect for God results in respect for all family-related functions.

Nurture Children in Spiritual Tradition

The Hebrew family played an important role in observing spiritual traditions, imparting convictions to children, and providing training in morals (Exod. 12:1–12; 13:7–10, 14; Lev. 18; Deut. 5–6; 11:1–7, 9, 21; 16:11–12; 28:49–57; 31:13). Nothing could be more instructive than young children watching their father slay a lamb and make preparations for Passover (Exod. 12:3). The transmission of the faith and traditions of faith were a requirement placed upon each hearer and experiencer of God's Word.

Maintain Both Family Solidarity and Individual Freedom

God orders a balance between maintaining family solidarity while allowing individual rights and choices (Exod. 21:3–11; Deut. 24:16; 25:5). If a man died without having a son to continue his name, his closest relative had the obligation of taking the man's wife as his own and raising up an heir both for her and the name of her dead husband. This act did more than just maintain property rights within the family; it was an act of family solidarity as well as compassion for the widow. On issues of individual sin, however, each family member bore his own responsibility and not that of the entire family. "Each is to die for his own sin" (Deut. 24:16). God's revelation concerning the importance of family solidarity does not negate the importance of individual justice and choices. Here Scripture provides a unique balance between family commitment to unity and individual freedom.

Maintain a Unique Sexuality

God makes it clear to the Hebrew people that the sexual practices they will encounter when they enter the land of Canaan are forbidden to them as people of God. Such things as nakedness, adultery, infanticide, homosexuality, and bestiality are all condemned (Lev. 18). There are also instructions about seminal emissions and menstrual periods (Lev. 15). Apparently, God was concerned that his people conduct their sexual lives in unique ways: monogamous, ritually pure, heterosexual, and not with close relatives (unless by the law of raising up offspring to a dead relative).

Do Justice to Nonfamily Members

God also commands his concern for outsiders; healthy families are not to be turned in on themselves. They are to concern themselves with the less fortunate outside their walls, specifically widows, the poor, aliens, the fatherless, and the stranger (Exod. 22:22; Lev. 19:10, 34; Deut. 15:4–11; 24:20; 25:5).

Respect Authority

Respect for parents, in-laws, and elders is emphasized and required of the Hebrews (Exod. 18:11–27; 20:12; Lev. 19:3). New marriages are granted an exemption from military service (Deut. 20:7); thus the authority of the newlywed relationship takes precedence over serving the nation.

Differentiate Gender

By today's feminist standards, many Old Testament laws about gender differences seem biased; apparently God did not want his people to be confused about their sexual identity. Leviticus, in particular, regulates women's purity and men's purity differently. Likewise, the law condemns homosexuality and the wearing of opposite sex apparel (Deut. 22:5).

Shared Spirituality

The final important trait noted during this age is that marriages and families were to be rooted in a shared spiritual value system (Exod. 34:16; Num. 25:1; Deut. 2:9–14; 7:3). God prohibited the Israelites from marrying those who did not share the same God and the same spiritual convictions. The Canaanites worshiped different gods, so intermarriage was forbidden with the people of the land. In addition, Hebrew children were to be taught the history, standards, and values of their nation. It was expected that parents be the purveyors of this spiritual heritage imparting commands, ordinances, and statutes to the next generation. The assumption is clear. God's design for the family was for each member of the household to embrace belief in one God and to adopt his commands and ordinances into personal life.

Family Dynamics of the Monarchy Period

Leading up to the period of Israel's kings, we see in the Book of Joshua the importance of visible memorials to educate children (Josh. 4:6–24) as well as the importance of family commitment to God (24:25). During the period of the judges, a severe moral decline is evident due to rampant sexual unfaithfulness: marrying Canaanite wives, multiplication of wives, and using concubines and prostitutes. During this period, only the Book of Ruth offers a positive picture of family life where maintaining family property or family legacy and caring for living descendants demonstrates high regard for the family as a unit, including nonblood relations. By contrast, ignoring relatives, their property, or the family name is to disrespect the family. The importance of family solidarity and support is central to the Book of Ruth.

During the monarchy period, Israel as a small shepherd people reached incredible grandeur. During the production of the wisdom literature, some of the finest family education materials were written, but when narrative portions are studied, little wisdom is observed in real life. Knowing what one should do to enhance family health is far different than actually doing it! I have often said I know far more biblical truth than I can ever fulfill! But I have distilled seven critical aspects to healthy families during the monarchy period.

Parents Nurture Children

The wisdom literature, especially Proverbs, underscores the importance of parental discipline, nurture, and education while narrative portions illustrate the results of their absence. The active involvement of parents in the lives of children giving direction, correction, and affection is paramount. Kidner calls Proverbs "an education in life as taught by one with fatherly wisdom."[5] As such, these "fatherly talks" press home the choices young people must make between wisdom and folly (Prov. 1:8; 2:1; 3:1; 5:1; 10:1; 13:1). A child left to himself brings shame to his parents (29:15). Childhood discipline and education form the emphasis equally (22:6, 15; 23:22; 29:17; 30:11–12).

Children Respect Parents

The flipside of the above has to do with a child's respect for his parents. Throughout Proverbs, children are admonished to obey their parents and heed their correction. The rod of discipline is not to be rejected by the child, and the rebellious child is presented as having a difficult life, perhaps leading to death (Prov. 29:17; 22:15; 20:20). Narrative portions of Scripture during this time highlight the principle that undisciplined sons like Absalom become destructive forces not only to their parents, but also to the nation.

Parental Failure Affects Children

The first two principles lead to a third one. During the monarchy period, the decalogue truth of the sins of the fathers visiting successive generations (Exod. 20:5) is seen graphically in the failure of Eli, David's neglect of Absalom, and Solomon's extreme sensuality. Periodically, exceptions to the rule are noted where God's marvelous grace is extended to an individual, bringing about significant changes (Hezekiah, Josiah). Today, family systems theory is just recognizing the impact of "sins of the fathers" upon children and grandchildren.

Marital Sexuality Is Positive

Proverbs, Ecclesiastes, and the Song of Songs all teach the importance of a positive sexual experience in marriage (Prov. 5:15–20; Eccles. 9:9; Song of Songs 8:6–8). A positive sexual experience is set in definite contrast to illicit sexual activity that can cost one's life (Prov. 7:1–23). Monogamous relationships are encouraged and the use of prostitutes and involvement in adulterous relationships are forbidden. Historical narrative sections confirm this instruction through negative illustrations. Consistently, Israel's greatest leaders had their downfall through illicit sexual relations: David with Bathsheba, Absalom with David's concubines, and Solomon with his hundreds of wives and concubines. It is better to enjoy life with the wife of one's youth than to face the reality that all is vanity!

Marriage Is Valued

A sixth aspect to this period involves the high ethical regard marriage is given as rooted in the divine resources of faith and commitment. Proverbs emphasizes the cherished value of the "good" wife as a gift from the Lord, along with the virtue of the "righteous" man. Without these resources, marriage can be painful or vain. When Israel's kings intermarried and committed adultery, the conclusion is drawn that they first forsook their God.

God, Home, and Society Are Inseparable

Also during the monarchy period, there seems to be an inseparable relationship between the home, the larger society, and God. Faithfulness to God builds and preserves the home, which in turn strengthens society. In this development, it is difficult to observe which comes first: failure in the home or failure with one's God, but the connection exists. The home reflects the larger society and the home impacts and creates the larger world. This interactional dependency is what makes for a delicate relationship. But one thing is clear: When the home departs from God, society will soon follow.

Prophetic Period Family Dynamic

During the prophetic period, the subject of the family is only marginally addressed, usually in the context of some failure within the nation of Israel. The fundamental mission of the prophets was to play the antagonist in Israel's decline and be the divine conscience about issues of faithfulness, justice, and equity. The historical books of the period (Ezra, Nehemiah, and Esther) promote the importance of racially pure marriages (Ezra 9:1–14; 10:3, 17). Likewise, Nehemiah commands the shunning of interracial marriages as a requirement for signing a new pledge of faithfulness (Neh. 10:28–29). In addition, Nehemiah condemns high interest rates (usury), and commands that property held at interest be returned. The prophet's concern is the kingdom of God and how national political conditions, including family issues, illustrate the nation's turning from God. From this period, five characteristics can be observed.

Permanence and Purity of Marriage

First, the permanence and purity of the marriage relationship is reinforced. From Isaiah to Malachi, the prohibitions of marriage with non-Israelites argued for the importance of the spiritual purity of marriage.[6] Through the prophet Malachi, God made clear the permanence of marriage when "I hate divorce" is thundered by the Lord himself (Mal. 2:16). The illustration of Hosea's unfailing love toward Gomer, a harlot, equally underscores God's attitude toward the commitment of a husband to a wife. Marriage in this sense is a covenant, rooted in an unconditional loyalty and mercy that only God can provide and command (Mal. 2:14).

Divine Nature of Marriage

Also during this time is the consistent usage of the marriage metaphor to illustrate God's relation to Israel. This reaffirms the spiritual connection between marriage and God. Both are based on a covenant relation, both are spiritual in nature, and both are unconditional. For good reason this relationship is picked up by the apostle Paul in the New Testament to illustrate Christ's relation to the church, and the relation of a husband to his wife. The spiritual and marital dynamics are so intertwined in Scripture that one is constantly used to illustrate the other. As such, marriage is truly a divine, spiritual institution.

Individual Responsibility

A fourth dynamic revealed during this period is the role of individual responsibility in the family. Parents' claiming Proverbs 22:6, "Train a child in the way he should go, and when he is old he will not turn from it," is problematic. Though parents are the foremost agents in the nurture of children, they cannot bear exclusive responsibility for their children's rebellion or failure. At every point in the child's developmental journey he or she is making choices and must bear the responsibility for these choices. This reality should provide good news for parents who suffer the pain of rebellious children.

Concern for Those in Need

An increasing concern for those suffering from family loss or absence is prevalent throughout the prophetic period. Respect for widows, the poor, fatherless, in-laws, and aliens leads toward an understanding that the family should not be turned in on itself (Mal. 3:5; Zech. 7:10). In addition, unlawful interest rates are addressed and issues of justice in regard to family property are dealt with (Micah 2:1–2). The implication is clear: It is hard for families to be healthy under economic injustices and hardships. Correction of the problem begins in the prophetic word and not experts in law, or politicians!

Need for Messianic Intervention

The Old Testament canon concludes with a promise that family enmity will ultimately be resolved through a change of heart brought on by the prophetic work of the coming Elijah (Mal. 4:6). Apparently, since the depth of human sinfulness and failure in family life had reached a low point, only the miraculous work of this messianic figure could restore the breaches. This is the same conclusion I reached several years ago as a family counselor. One can teach all the right things about family health and work hard at establishing a happy home, but until one's heart is changed, the best therapy and the most passionate desire is of no avail!

Old Testament Themes

It is difficult to pull together everything the Old Testament says about family functioning, but several themes reemerge.

Marital Fidelity

The most obvious principle for healthy family life is the centrality of a monogamous, sexually faithful husband-and-wife relationship. Although polygamy, concubines, and prostitutes existed in the lives of biblical characters, these were never the ideal and their practice inevitably had destructive effects. Hans Walter Wolff agrees:

> Thus the Old Testament is perfectly frank about the varied disorders and threats to man in his status as created being, and the love relationship founded on that status. It describes these disturbances as clearly as it describes the rapture of the whole union of love. It is always a disturbance in the relationship to God which shows itself . . . in different ways in the disturbance within the common life of man and woman.[7]

Relationships of Responsibility and Respect

The parent-child relationship is one of responsibility and respect whereby both parents have equal share in the nurturing and disciplining functions. The upbringing of children is the task of both parents (Deut. 8:5; Prov. 1:8; 6:20; 31:1) and not a strict role type for just one gender. Parents are responsible to protect and provide for their children as well as they can, knowing full well that only God can fully protect and provide for any human being (Job 5:4; Ps. 62:5–8; Prov. 14:26). Children are to respect their parents (Prov. 23:22), and when they become adults, they are responsible to care and provide for their parents (Ruth; Prov. 19:26).

Social Justice

The Old Testament theme of social justice extends equally to family life. The family has a responsibility to be concerned about the external community and issues of justice in the lives of its neighbors. The message of the prophets exhorts the importance of seeing justice done for widows, orphans, and aliens. Even relatives by marriage are to be given due respect and protection under the laws of Israel (Exod. 22:21; Deut. 16:11; Zech. 7:10).

Reality of Family Conflict

The Old Testament is one of the most realistic documents in the world; its graphic portrayal of human weakness, violence, and sin is unique among sacred literature of the world. Thus, what is taught about family life is realistic. Family conflict should not surprise anyone—the Bible is full of it. Marriages have problems, and sometimes the family system almost destroys the individuals from within. Patriarchs to prophets, the family does not do that well.

Necessity of Divine Intervention and Resources

Finally, the constant need for divine intervention is seen in the Old Testament. Just as God intervened when he saw the aloneness of the first male, so he must intervene for fallen man in a fallen environment. The family left to itself builds paneled houses, compounds wives, has affairs, rebels against parents, and splits itself right down the seams. Malachi ends his prophetic ministry with both the need and promise for intervention—an intervention from God. Where the Old Testament ends, the New Testament begins—with one who can change the *source* of all human conflict, the human heart!

5

What the Bible Says about Families in the New Testament

The New Testament opens with the coming of the Messiah and his forerunner, Elijah (John the Baptist). With this divine intervention, a tension is immediately created between human potentiality and human reality. On the one hand, the Messiah offers the good news of the kingdom that potentially will turn the hearts of parents toward children and of wives and husbands toward each other. On the other hand, the same gospel message becomes a sword and causes division in the most intimate of family relationships.

This invasion of God via the incarnation sets the stage for a New Testament doctrine of the family during the church age. Great potential exists for family health while the realism of family strife remains a constant. Beginning with Christ's teaching and with further clarification by the apostles (particularly Paul and Peter), family doctrine takes on new clarity and importance. Hazen G. Werner comments:

> The Christian family and its activity and relationships began a new tradition in the pagan world. There came into

> being a design of life, customs, and practices that marked the Christian family with certain distinctions. The Christian family was different in its way of life, its ethical standards, its regard for others, the respect which members of the family held for one another, and its faith in God.[1]

What Jesus and his apostles accomplished was to bring the subject of family life under the scrutiny of God's kingdom purposes. In the process, many existing standards and values were threatened while followers of Christ learned to live differently in the family context.

The First Family

The first family of the New Testament is, of course, Mary and Joseph. We know little about them, and Joseph drops completely out of sight after the Jesus narrative. Some have argued Joseph is not mentioned during the adult life of Christ because he must have died, leaving Mary as a single mother with several children (Matt. 12:46). Jesus as an adult son places his own biological family in a secondary position to the spiritual relationships among his followers. Jesus affirms the continuing care for his mother (John 19:27) while teaching that "a man's enemies will be the members of his own household" (Matt. 10:36). If anything, Jesus' "traditional" family was superceded by those desiring to do his father's will. Even though he had a biological family living in a house in Nazareth, he claimed, "The Son of Man has no place to lay his head" (Matt. 8:20).

Family Teaching in the Gospels

Under the tutelage of their Lord, Jesus' followers and observers understood that the institution of marriage was to be permanent. Jesus concluded that divorce constituted adultery in most cases and was not justified for one of his followers (Matt. 19:1–12; Mark 10:2–12). There is lengthy debate on whether Jesus allowed any divorce and remarriage; however, it is not my purpose to give an answer to this problem. I will refer the reader to extensive literature on the subject.[2]

In arguing for permanence of marriage, Jesus refers to the original creation design (Matt. 19). While affirming the ideal, he transcends it by teaching the concept of the spiritual family (Matt. 12:46–50; Mark 3:31–35). This new family of God consists of those who do the will of God, thus creating new earthly family relations. Earthly relations are not to have precedence over one's relationship to Christ (Matt. 10:34–38; Luke 14:26), and doing God's will inevitably brings the believer into conflict with his earthly family (Luke 12:13–21). Christ demands to be Lord of the home and of the marriage relationship. Jesus affirmed the authority and honor of parents in the family relationship, but he did not make this the highest principle of family authority. This is an important concept in light of the "chain of command" view of authority that restricts young adults from pursuing God's call on their life apart from parental consent. Jesus made it clear that this tension would exist, and when it does his calling must come first (Mark 6:3–5; 12:13–17).

Jesus exalted the status of women and children while he did not appear as a social reformer arguing the case of women and children at every turn. In his relations with women and children, he modeled a surprisingly novel behavior by breaking down serious cultural barriers. He spoke with a Samaritan woman (John 4:7) and healed a Syrophoenecian woman's demon-possessed daughter (Mark 7:24–30) and an "unclean" woman with the issue of blood (5:25–34).

In demonstrating equality toward all kinds of people, Jesus rejected the prejudices of society and laid a groundwork for instruction by the apostles. Though he radically defended women and children and his impact upon them was significant (Mark 9:42), Jesus did not call women or children to be his disciples. He maintained a delicate balance between fundamental human equality while maintaining social sexual differences.

Lastly, and probably most important, Jesus rooted family conflict in the realm of the human heart (Matt. 5:21–28). This idea is especially profound in light of current trends to see family problems as management problems, system dysfunction, role confusion, or political agenda items. Some say, "If we can restore the family to its proper order or get more money for family problems, then things will be better." My response is a simple "Not." These superficial organizational solutions to complex issues are like rearranging deck chairs on the *Titanic.* It may make some people feel better (for doing *something*), but the ship is going down. Jesus called the Pharisees' solutions "whitewashing" that make dead men look better (Matt. 23:27; Mark 7:14–23). A role approach to family life does not go deeply enough, nor does it address our spiritual nature. There is a lot of "Christian" family therapy going on today that is no more than whitewashing of diseased hearts.

The Family in the Acts of the Apostles

Though it does not record direct teaching about family life, the Book of Acts depicts the family as becoming a center for church ministry and evangelism. Couples and households are vitally important in providing a base of operations for Christian ministry. Baptisms of entire households argue for a solidarity of faith throughout the entire family (Acts 16:33). Priscilla and Aquila, a married couple apparently without children, offer one of the most outstanding ministries in the New Testament, predominately through the influence of their home (18:1–11, 18, 22; see also 1 Cor. 16:19; Rom. 16:3–5; 2 Tim. 4:19). What is clear in the Book of Acts is that couples and individuals used their homes as places from which to reach out while also inviting outsiders in. These homes are anything but isolated castles protecting the family from outside influences. Families are involved, engaged, and assertive as shining lights in a dark world.

During the early church, the overall movement is twofold. First, the apostles in teaching and preaching the "things concerning the kingdom of God" (see Acts 1:3; 28:31) demonstrated how God is incorporating into the church a people of every race, status, and gender. Hellenistic Jews were included into the spiritual fellowship at Pentecost (Acts 2) followed by a lame beggar (3:2), an Ethiopian eunuch (8:27), a Roman centurion (10:4), various Gentiles (13:48), a businesswoman (16:14), a Roman jailer (16:30), and of course, the greatest persecutor of the new religion, Saul (9:6).

A second aspect to the early church movement was how homes became the locale of evangelism and fellowship. The home was no longer exclusively a place of nurture for one biological family or extended family, but for the family of God, the church. The values of the kingdom would now take precedence over the values of "traditional" family structures. Mary, the mother of Jesus, and her other children were incorporated into the larger spiritual congregation (Acts 1:14). A married couple, Ananias and Sapphira, were severely judged for lying to the Holy Spirit in regard to a private property issue (5:4). Timothy, a key player in the early church, is the product of an interracial marriage (16:1). When the gospel of the kingdom took hold of an individual's life, the transformation affected entire households, resulting in the baptism of all (16:14–15, 33). Aquila and Priscilla, Jewish believers from Pontus, used their home as a place for apostolic hospitality, instruction, and worship (Acts 18:3, 11; 1 Cor. 16:5).

Paul's Teaching on Family

Christianity, by its basic nature, must be lived out in the totality of one's life; if Christ is Lord, he is Lord of all. But the early church, while making Jesus Lord of their lives, needed further clarification on how their faith should be reflected in marital and family relations. Paul addresses these concerns directly or indirectly in all his letters. He, more than any other apostle, had the difficult task of relating the truth of the new evangelical faith to all areas of life, including the family. Paul is both the best known and the most misunderstood theologian of the early church. His instruction brought controversy that continues to this day.

Throughout the early church period the significance of marriage also changes. The apostle Paul as a single or widowed missionary argues his own single state is a better alternative for the expansion of the gospel. Singleness allows freedom from the normal marital constraints (1 Cor. 7:8, 32–33, 40). However, if a person chooses to marry, marriage and family life should be exemplary in order for that person to be considered for leadership in the church (1 Tim. 3:2–5). Family responsibilities are still affirmed in terms of care of older parents, one's own children, and widows (1 Tim. 5:3–8). Marriage is affirmed by Paul (1 Cor. 7:2, 28; Titus 2:3–5), but not with the high sanctity that the institution will achieve in later years when it becomes a sacrament. Marriage is an option of choice in the service of Christ, but not a requirement. Paul prefers older widows to remain as they are unless they can't control their sexual desires (1 Cor. 7:8–9).

As a new Christian, I was immediately struck by how Paul uses the family metaphor throughout his writings. He calls God Father and Christ God's Son; all believers are "sons" of God; and the church is made up of brothers and sisters. In other words, Paul sees the church as a community intertwining the spiritual and family relationships. Family concepts inform the spiritual. Spiritual concepts feed the family. This is clarification of Jesus' original teaching, "Who is my family?"

Paul continues the affirmation of the permanency, fidelity, and realism of the marriage relationship. He affirms marriage "till death do us part" (Rom. 7) while recognizing marriages are lived out in the context of changing contemporary problems. Some believers are married to unbelievers, some are single, and some have already remarried (1 Cor. 7). His thinking on marital infidelity is clear as illustrated by his admonitions against sexual immorality (1 Cor. 5; 1 Thess. 4) mixed with pointed encouragement of sexual expression in the context of marriage. Marriage cannot claim to be "Christian" where infidelity exists, and a healthy sexual relationship is a strong preventive and antidote in a sexually permissive culture (1 Cor. 7:1–5). Without lovemaking any marriage is at risk.

The apostle Paul outlines clear, reciprocal, but differing responsibilities in the marriage relationship, addressing these on the basis of gender. His primary goal is creating harmony and unity through complementary responsibilities. Clark writes, "The text (Eph. 5:22–33) has a practical function in regard to marriage. It does not exalt the married couple, but rather instructs them in their marriage. Moreover, the goal of this family order is unity, an internal oneness that allows the family to be an effective cell in the Christian community."[3]

The husband's responsibility focuses on sacrificial love, direction, and nurture (Eph. 5:23–28). The wife's responsibility centers on submission, love, and respect (Eph. 5:22, 33; Titus 2:4). At the functional level, these make for a reciprocal relationship where each party receives what they need in order to be loved and affirmed. When either begins to demand what the other is supposed to give or is not willing to give, the relationship breaks down. Neither party can function healthfully until its reciprocal nature is restored. The basic traits will be mutual sacrificial loyalty, authority, and equality (1 Cor. 11:1–16 and Gal. 3:26–29), essentially a relationship of constant acquiescence. Mike Mason writes, "Nowhere is the issue of acquiescence to the will of another more germane. No compliance is more personal or more necessary than that required in marriage."[4]

Paul's parent-child dichotomy is never confused. A relationship of authority exists, but never in a tyrannical way. In fact, it seems Paul is more concerned about the harm that can be done to children through too much control than merely having them under the control of the parent. Fathers are especially cautioned not to cause their children to "lose heart" or become "embittered" because of extreme parental authority or discipline (Eph. 6:4; Col. 3:21). If control cannot be accomplished without a sense of the child's fundamental human dignity, then control amounts to nothing (1 Tim. 3:4). Mothers are seen as providing affection (1 Thess. 2:7; Titus 2:4) while the father is admonished to give education, correction (Eph. 6:4), and direction to the child.

I assert my opinion again that these admonitions and imperatives don't amount to maintaining particular roles or structures, nor should they result in a system of rules. These are simply responsibilities that will allow the Christian family to function in a harmonious way under the lordship of Christ.

Finally, Paul goes to the heart of family functioning. Without addressing the issues of the human spirit, commands and imperatives may do more harm than good. Characteristic of Paul's writings is that he never asks the reader to do something before he has offered substantial rationale for doing it. For example, in the Book of Ephesians, he spends almost five chapters out of six revealing the depths of what Christ has accomplished in regard to our salvation. There is not one imperative or command until chapter 4, verse 1, where he asks the reader to walk in a manner worthy of Christ. The implication seems obvious: Until we understand fully what Christ has accomplished for us, and the manner in which he did it, we cannot understand how to implement the family responsibilities God desires. Christ and the Holy Spirit of God are Paul's rationale, source, and motivation for family instruction. This suggests that marital and parental responsibilities are not arbitrary in Paul's mind, but specifically informed by his larger theology. They are not rooted in some cultural consensus or contemporary research, but in the totality of Paul's understanding of the person and work of Christ.

Without a clear understanding of Christology, pneumology, and soteriology, Paul's doctrine of the family falls to pieces. This approach to the family has nothing to do with how often one goes to church, who takes out the garbage, or whether our kids go to Christian schools. What makes a family Christian has to do with Christ and his example. Paul never separated family teaching from the rest of his theology of the incarnate Christ. He is not offering grandfatherly practical advice to moms and dads about what works, but godly wisdom rooted in the actions and attitudes of Jesus Christ.

Though Paul was not a social reformer or family advocate, his concepts of a healthy family brought significant change in the larger society. Someone once said that by the end of the first century Romans were calling their sons Paul and their dogs Nero! The apostle's goal lies in building relationships grounded in specific responsibilities that in turn create unity under the lordship of Christ. The key to marriage lies in a couple's recognition of Christ as their example and power. Donald Guthrie summarizes: "Inherent in Paul's approach were principles which could not fail to have some impact on society as soon as Christianity grew strong enough to make its influence felt."[5]

Since Paul is sometimes claimed as the author of Hebrews, I will deal with one short passage from that book.[6] The clearest reference in the Book of Hebrews about family functioning is in chapter 13, verse 4, where the text states, "Marriage should be honored by all, and the marriage bed kept pure, for God will judge the adulterer and all the sexually immoral." The author is affirming the universal respect that should be given to the marriage state along with the necessity of maintaining sexual fidelity. The word for marriage bed is literally "intercourse" *(koite),* meaning the place of intercourse.[7] What the writer is admonishing is the outright refusal to make the bed a place of fornication and adultery. The brief passage then affirms the honor of marriage and the sanctity of the sexual relationship. Violators face a severe personal judgment from God.

Peter's Teaching on Healthy Families

If Paul looks at the family through the lens of a single man, the apostle Peter views it from the married perspective (Mark 1:30; 1 Cor. 9:5). The result of a comparison yields several insightful differences.

Peter addresses wives by emphasizing their inward spirit in concert with outward submission (1 Peter 3:1–6), similar to Paul's instruction. However, Peter adds a new dynamic for husbands. He asks husbands to "dwell with their wives on the basis of understanding" or knowledge (Greek, *kata gnosin*), very much a married man's insight. Almost every woman desires better communication from her husband, and as we know, most men don't do it that well. Here, Peter zeros in on one of the most significant problems in marriage; apparently couples in the first century encountered the same issues couples experience in the twenty-first!

The rationale Peter offers for husbands to talk more is threefold: First, because their wives are "weaker vessels." This weakness is hotly debated and often found offensive; the meaning, in fact, is not exact. The word for weakness, *astheneteros,* combined with the word for vessel, *skeous,* meaning jar, may contain the more positive idea of sensitivity and fragility, as in a precious antique vase.[8]

The second reason men need to communicate more with their wives is because wives are women! This implies they have a completely different style of communicating, proven in recent years by considerable research.[9] Here, Peter confronts the fundamental male/female differences that confound so many marriages. A husband needs to communicate with his wife so she can better understand what he is like as a man, and he can understand her femininity on a broader level.

A third reason to communicate more involves the husband's prayer life. As difficult and unfair as this seems, Peter's text claims that a man's prayer life is proportionate to his investment in understanding his wife. A man needs to communicate lest his prayers be hindered. No comparable command or rationale is given to the wife, probably because she comes by communication much more naturally.

Peter's instruction also notes the importance of husbands treating their wives with respect and honor rooted in the concept that they are "fellow heirs of the grace of life." In other words, men and women share in God's grace and gifts. The concept of being co-heirs implies equality of status. The wife is still to submit to her husband, implying that subordination be offered as an equal in God's grace. Again, we notice the reciprocal nature of the relationship. She submits to his authority while he honors and respects her as a co-heir with equal authority. The key facilitating dynamic that enables this kind of relationship is communication, communication, and more communication.

Before addressing these family functions, Peter reminds his readers that all believers have been called to the sufferings of Christ and are admonished to follow in his footsteps. It is then Christ's work of redemption on the cross that provides the example, incentive, and power to fulfill marital responsibilities (1 Peter 3:21–25).

In Peter's second letter, only one verse addresses the family, referring to false prophets filled with sensuality and eyes full of adultery (2 Peter 2:14). This merely confirms the consistent emphasis on sexual fidelity alongside the recognition that sexual predators exist even within the church. These people lie in the name of God and violate marriages by using the trusted brother-sister relationship to fulfill their own appetites.

John's Teaching on Family Health

The beloved disciple John does not directly address family issues but does use family metaphors to describe the believer's spiritual relationships. John assumes the family connection among all believers (1 John 1:2) and especially emphasizes the responsibility each believer has to others in the family (1 John 2:10; 3:17). He uses the father-son relationship to illustrate the relationship believers have with their heavenly Father (3:1–3) and the father-son relationship to illustrate the relationship between older and younger believers (John 2:12–14). From this perspective, Christian marriage is the ultimate brother-sister relationship in the Lord.

John's Book of Revelation uses marriage and family metaphors to describe the apocalyptic vision. It pictures the return of Christ as a ceremonial marriage supper (Rev. 19:7–9), while the New Jerusalem comes down from God as a bride adorned for her husband (21:2). These passages underscore cultural norms: the marriage supper is a time of celebration; a bride desires to get dressed up for her husband.

Just as the Old Testament ended with a forward-looking motif, so does the New. As Malachi looked for the time when parents and children would turn their hearts back toward each other, so Revelation ends looking to a grand reunion with Christ. In this sense, our Elijah is yet to come—the one who will turn our hearts fully to Christ. Until then, we have the instruction manual from Scripture that gives us guidance in our fallen state. Faithfully fulfilling biblical responsibilities does not ensure we will not have family problems or serious strife. But as we seek to do God's will in this world, we have the promise that we are his family. Equally, as we strive to live in accord with these responsibilities we have the satisfaction of knowing we are fulfilling our side of the bargain. I cannot make my wife love, respect, or submit to me. (Believe me, I have tried!) But I can seek to love her sacrificially. Satisfaction comes in knowing that I have done my part!

Family Life Deemphasized

From this survey, it seems the teaching of the early church on the subject of the family is far different from what we find today. If anything, New Testament marriage is somewhat deemphasized while the single state is soundly legitimized. As Clapp observes, "To put it strongly, there is at least one sure sign of a flawed vision of the Christian family: it denigrates and dishonors singleness."[10] In Jewish culture, marriage was a religious duty, but beginning with the unmarried Jesus a significant shift of emphasis takes place. Natural family relationships are now secondary to doing the will of God. The focus is no longer on the earthly family but the kingdom of God and being a member of God's household (Eph. 2:19). If anything, to focus on the family in New Testament times means focusing on the family of God! This focus, however, does not involve a new model for family life. There are no common family life models in the New Testament. Instead of models, certain functions are affirmed in order to regulate Christian relations under the lordship of Christ.

While affirming the legitimacy and normality of biological family relations, the New Testament does not exalt these relationships or make them into Christian ideals. There are no perfect family models in the Bible. Because of the continuing presence of sin, family relationships must be regulated in the spirit and admonition of Christ (Eph. 5–6; 1 Cor. 7; Col. 3; 1 Peter 3:1–7). Each admonition and imperative asks the individual hearer to respond to their partner or parent in a distinctively Christian fashion. In every command, Christ is the issue, example, and focus. Wives are to submit to their husbands as unto the Lord; husbands are to love their wives as Christ does the church; children are to obey their parents as an expression of pleasing Christ. Some would like to see a traditional hierarchy here, but in my opinion everyone has the same "role": to be in subordination to Christ. Subordination for the Christian is not just the responsibility of wives or children, but of everyone! As the apostle says, "submit to one another out of reverence for Christ" (Eph. 5:21). This is not the result of submitting to some ordered structure or set of rules, but a response born in grace and submission to the Holy Spirit of God (Eph. 5:18).

What God Desires: Seven Keys to a Healthy Family

The White House Working Group on the Family called the family (in the words of Edmund Burke) "The little platoon we belong to as the first principle of public affections."[11] I believe Scripture gives us a target at which to aim these affections, but it's only a target, not a guarantee. To be healthy we need to understand not only the letter of our biblical responsibilities but also their spirit.

1. Respect in All Relationships

When I first began this study, I was amazed because I expected to find in my research emphasis on marital communication and intimacy. What surprised me most was the consistent emphasis, instead, on respect in literally every human relationship. I was also amazed how Scripture affirms this function in family life, beginning with respect and honor for God. Likewise, husbands are to respect their wives as co-heirs, wives are to respect their husbands, parents are to grant dignity to their children, and children are to honor their parents. Respect is to be shown to those who are elders while elders are to treat the younger Christians as sons as well as brothers and sisters (1 Tim. 5:1–2). In addition, respect is to be shown to those outside the home: Widows, orphans, aliens, neighbors, and Christian brothers and sisters are to be given the kind of treatment that expresses universal inherent human worth. This respect for every human life regardless of age, gender, race, or status is rooted in the creation mandate of the divine image, or *imago dei.* Though severely defaced by human sinfulness, the image of God in all mankind is not erased; it becomes the rationale for all respect.

In biblical terminology, respect means to grant significance, weight, or value. In other words, because every human being is valuable to God, they should be valuable to you and me. A family that desires to live by biblical wisdom is then a family that honors every member of the human family and grants dignity to each. But what will this look like?

When two human beings produce offspring, the genetic possibilities are legion. I was somewhat naïve about this when my children arrived on the scene. I expected some differences but had no idea how different my children would be. Not only were they different from each other, but they were also utterly different from me! That's what it means to be made in the image of God, each human being a unique person. The downside of this involves accepting incredibly disorienting differences, some of which are downright annoying. Clapp humorously observes, "Christians have children so we can become the kind of people who welcome strangers."[12] But it only begins with children. Welcoming "aliens" is the essence of what it means to respect the differences found in the human family. Accepting the reality that everyone is unlike me is quite a stretch. It would be so much easier if others conformed to our personality, expectations, dress, and opinions. But respect asserts the honor of differing personalities, opinions, tastes, and psychological boundaries.

What one person perceives as close, another may perceive as smothering. Respect grants emotional rope to tolerate diversity. Of course, one of the problems today is that God's grand idea of diversity has become politicized. It is required by law in the workplace, but in truth it is rooted in a theology of the image of God. How can we accept human beings who are not like us apart from understanding them as equally valuable and worthy because they, too, are made in God's image?

I don't always do well at respect, but at least I know what I should do. I have struggled with my kids wanting tattoos, not finishing college, and being artistic when I wanted them to be literary. I have struggled living with an extrovert wife when I often preferred to stay home and read. It's been a serious step for me to respect a family relative who has chosen a gay lifestyle.

Respect also means that clear responsibilities are maintained and that children grant parents the authority due their position. I admire my wife in this regard; though her biological father lived far away and rarely communicated, she stayed in contact and made sure all family news reached him. She felt a responsibility to honor her father in spite of distance, divorce, and disease. Likewise, parents are not to lord it over their children, thus destroying the child's spirit. Paul made clear the potential fathers have to exasperate their children so that they "lose heart" (Col. 3:21 NASB). A parent can suck the heart and spirit out of children merely by not granting them the dignity and honor due them. Anyone who has worked with abused children will quickly affirm this biblical truth. Researchers have shown the healthiest families demonstrate neither an authoritarian dominance nor a loose chaotic approach to power. The most unhealthy families are on the extremes.[13] This is precisely the balance Scripture admonishes.

2. Authority and Affection in Balance

How can authority coexist with affection? Husbands are commanded to love their wives, and wives, their husbands; yet in both responsibilities there is recognition of authority. Wives are to respect their husbands and be submissive. Husbands are to grant wives honor as joint-heirs and be willing to give themselves (submit) to their wives. Children are to obey parents, recognizing their authority. Parents are commissioned to love, nurture, and delight in their children (Prov. 3:12).[14] Scripturally, affectionate relationships flourish within authoritative guidelines.

My role as a military chaplain has helped me understand the tension of this relationship. In the Air Force, chaplains serve with officer rank but without command authority. When someone of lesser rank sees me walking down a base sidewalk, military custom requires them to initiate a salute, acknowledging my superior rank as an officer. However, were I to stop this person and say, "I want you to paint this building right now," he would have every right to tell me where to go. With the cross on my uniform I do not have command authority. If I want him to paint the building I have to work through the right channels to get permission, or form a relationship with him and try to persuade him to do it after normal duty hours. Though I have the rank of a lieutenant colonel, I cannot use my rank to command anyone. I have to build relationships and use the power of that to achieve my goals. The same is true in a healthy family dynamic. Because a parent or spouse has authority by virtue of position does not mean that commandeering is the best way to get things done. Occasionally, authority may be exercised, but in healthy families it is used as a last resort, and is usually an expression of an already failed relationship.

Affection is not opposed to authoritative guidelines in the home; both are needed, and both are biblical. Though this balance is ideal, the realism of family life suggests that the pendulum will regularly swing from one side to another. A family is never static. New pressures, needs, and situations challenge the family every day. If anything, recognizing that both affection and authority are necessary allows a family to consistently adjust to new exigencies. This may get difficult as a child hits adolescence because the growing teen is both child and adult. On some days, "adult" wisdom and judgment is a welcomed surprise to the parent; on other days, a kid's foolishness is enough to turn his mother's hair gray. So what is a parent to do? Grant affection when kids make good decisions and withhold it in the face of stupidity? I think not. What a teen needs is both affection and authority every single day. Some days, a child may need more affection than authority, while on other days more authoritative boundaries may be required. When does a parent know which one is more needed at the moment? Short answer: probably never! The longer answer is that every situation and every child is different; the better we know our children, the better we can discern the time for discipline or praise. What this concept does is frees parents from the static role of seeing themselves merely as disciplinarians. Depending upon the situation and the needs of a child, a parent possesses the joint tools of affection and authority.

The concept of respect argues for welcoming every family problem as a unique opportunity to readjust the family in some new direction. Even family difficulties may be respected, welcomed, and incorporated into family history. Mistakes will be made, authority may be abused, and affection can turn into a permissive lenience. But healthy families find ways to balance these two vitally important qualities. Being rooted and bounded by a larger value system is as a corrective measure for extremes.

3. Redemptive Value System

Families are composed of fallible creatures. Being fallible means we need heavy doses of forgiveness in order to foster gracious relationships. In the Old Testament the family value system was rooted in recognition and acceptance of each other as people redeemed by God through the Red Sea experience. Whenever God asked his people to do something in the arena of family living, he always went back to this experience for justification (Deut. 6:20–25). Social justice was rooted in the fact that Israel had been slaves in Egypt and family teaching centered on God's intervention redeeming his people. What was created in this intervention was a covenant community made up of individuals living in a relationship of shared spiritual values (Exod. 19:5).

In the New Testament, specific family responsibilities and imperatives are rooted in the redemptive work of Christ. Family responsibilities are justified by the example of Jesus and his supreme redemptive work on the cross. This overall value system permeates biblical responsibilities. I have often felt it is wrong to ask wives to submit to their husbands if they have little knowledge of Christ's redemptive work. The apostles did not offer solutions to "intimacy" problems for those who did not accept a Christ-oriented value system. Their admonitions were not quick-fix magic bullets to help people who did not know Christ or were not willing to do his will. Scripture contains admonitions given to Christian homes to help families who were committed to Christ. They were meant to understand that family behavior be based on his work and example. There are probably many non-Christian marriages where the husband is a better lover of his wife than in Christian marriages. Likewise, in many non-Christian cultures, wives are more submissive to their husbands than in Christian homes. I have known many non-Christian couples who appear to be doing better than many Christian couples; there may be many reasons for this. But when two Christians marry they form a redemptive community within the larger redemptive community of the church. The bedrock of this little platoon is the extreme mercy God has demonstrated in his covenental love and everlasting commitment. Their acceptance of this covenant provides the rationale and power for hanging in there when one partner has had it.

I'm committed to each of the relationships in my family because God is committed to me. That's what covenant means. Nick Stinnett calls commitment the most important trait of family life: "Although we are reluctant to pinpoint one characteristic because we believe all six are of vital importance, this one characteristic [commitment] could be considered the foundation on which the other characteristics are built."[15] Family researcher Urie Bronfenbrenner believes the single most important thing a father can give his children is his "irrational commitment." Asked what this means, he replied, "It means a father that is crazy about his kids for no other reason than they are his kids."[16] This sounds like the kind of love our heavenly Father has for us!

God's irrational commitment extended toward me empowers me with the tenacity I need when I'm ready to give up on one of my kids or walk out on my wife. Mason acknowledges that "a marriage lives, paradoxically, upon those almost impossible times when it is perfectly clear to two partners that nothing else but pure sacrificial love can hold them together."[17] God's commitment also reminds me that no matter how ugly or ungodly are those around me, he has been patient with me and I can in turn be patient. Biblical family admonitions for the family should not be taken out of their larger theological or redemptive context. They are not for non-Christians, nor are they motivational principles for business seminars. They are not cure-alls for complex family difficulties. Biblical admonitions must be understood in the context of God's redemptive love for mankind and the love of Christ for the redeemed.

4. Hopeful Realism

One of the things I hope my readers have noticed along this biblical journey is how realistically Scripture portrays the human condition. To say the least, the Old Testament's presentation of the people of God is not flattering. The New Testament equally presents the church as a fallen institution with a host of human problems. Only Jesus is cast in blameless, positive tones of righteousness, but even he is not without conflicts, misunderstandings, or enemies. At the same time, the Bible's realism does not lead to fatalism or pessimism. Alongside a realistic portrait of humanity lies hope.

Hopeful realism is the middle ground between idealism and pessimism. The Bible is full of ideals about family life—alongside examples of family failure. Its realism is easily explained by the fact of human depravity. Its idealism is rooted in faith and hope. God's purposes and hope for a better future lie at the heart of a healthy family. This makes believers either realistic idealists, idealistic realists, or as I prefer, hopeful realists.

Hopeful family realism should teach me not to be surprised when the worst that can happen happens. Just as rain falls on the just and the unjust, so hurricanes, cancer, unwanted pregnancies, AIDS, divorce, unemployment, and untimely death come upon believers. Christians are naïve if they think they are immune to such things simply because they pray and read their Bibles. History and experience show otherwise. When crises occur, the hopeful family faces the difficulty honestly but with superior resources: faith and hope.

Just as the Old Testament closed with the promise of Elijah who would bring family renewal, so the New Testament ends with the vision of Christ returning and restoring all things (Col. 1:20; Rev. 19:9). What is interesting is how many Christians really don't entertain hope in Christ. Oh, we say we do, then turn and look for hope in other places, often somewhere in the past. The assumption is if we can just get back to a traditional family model then our families will be stronger. This hope lies in a past that probably didn't even exist. This is not a Christian hope, only a romantic notion.

Some see the hope of family in political activism. This, too, is misguided. Trying to strengthen or protect the family through action committees is needed, but is not an authentic Christian hope. Even Moral Majority founder Jerry Falwell recently admitted, "I don't believe for one moment that any of them [politicians supporting the Christian right] will do what they say."[18] When dean of Regent University's School of Government, Kay James, was asked whether a change in political leadership could heal the moral and spiritual brokenness of the nation, she answered, "No."[19] Our hope does not lie in a better or a different government. The blessed hope of the church is not in thousands of Christians flooding Congress with letters or holding a rally on the Washington mall.[20] Oh yes, we want the government to support a particular family form or legitimize in law bourgeois middle-class values, but these things have nothing to do with Christianity. Our hope is a clear but long awaited one. As James says, "Be patient, then, brothers, until the Lord's coming" (James 5:7). In the meantime, our response is to be committed to a "long obedience in the same direction," a phrase made popular by Eugene Peterson.

Hope for the family does not lie in counselors, therapists, or political activists, though these have their place. Fallible, feeble-minded, mixed-up human beings often have conflicted motives and agendas. I can kiss my wife or run for office with all kinds of impure or mixed motives! The calling and effort of our family guardians in Congress is commendable, yet, they are not the guardians of my family. No counselor, politician, or Christian leader like Jim Dobson, Gary Bauer, Pat Robertson, or Jerry Falwell has ever shown up on my doorstep to help me through some family difficulty. I don't even expect them to, because it's not what they do.

Who *has* been there during the sleepless nights waiting the return of a teenager, trying to finance college, or figuring how to make it through the next week? The Lord! I fall on my knees and ask God's strength and guidance for whatever it is I am dealing with. Then I get up and try to meet my responsibilities as a Christian father and husband. The only pure hope I have is in the establishment of Christ's kingdom on earth.

When I think about the future I am hopeful—not because the economy is good or we have the right people in government or because my family is doing reasonably well—I am hopeful in the biblical promise that Jesus is the same yesterday, today, and forever (Heb. 13:8). One day soon, if not later, I will meet him face to face!

5. Divine Intervention

God's first act of creation was to create order out of the murky waters of chaos (Gen. 1:2). When human violence filled the land, God intervened (6:5). When human faithfulness had reached a low ebb, God took a pagan idol worshiper and made a great nation for himself (12:1). When this family-nation disobeyed, God sent plagues and prophets to get its attention. He finally sent them his own son (Heb. 1:1–2). The conclusion is inescapable. Without the consistent intervention of God into human affairs, human and family decline is inevitable. Parents, teachers, and politicians who are doing the best they can are not enough. Ultimately God must break into a child's life, a parent's life, redeeming the soul and renewing the mind. Without this intervention, all a parent or teacher can do is to be the best model he or she can be. But how can any parent or spouse be what he or she should be? To be all we can possibly be would necessitate being divine, and I lack this quality. Whether it is in trying to be the best husband or the best parent, I will fail, sometimes big time! This is why we must see the family as a redemptive community enjoying the forgiveness and riches of God's grace (Eph. 1:7).

I always enjoy the process of facilitating premarital counseling. Young couples with that knocked-dead romance in their eyes are a wondrous sight indeed. But I usually feel sort of sorry for them; most have no idea what they are getting themselves into. To get their attention, I tell them marriage is like someone giving you a brand new Mercedes-Benz. It's shiny, beautiful, loaded with horsepower, AC, stereo speakers, audiotape, CDs, and power-everything. There is just one problem. There are no keys to the car. The wife gets inside to steer. The husband pushes from behind. Occasionally, they have to enlist someone else to help while they both push the shining car around a corner or up a hill. Every so often, one thinks, *Gee, owning a Mercedes is not what I thought it would be,* but never is a word of doubt spoken to the other. Finally, with clothes tattered and sweat soaking through, they jointly confess, "This isn't working; we need to ditch the car." I ask the obvious question, "What did this Mercedes need?"

The starry-eyed couple replies, "A key."

If marriage is a divine institution and not of human origin, then it will take divine resources to make it work. Christian marriage and families necessitate consistent divine direction and intervention. Without them, a couple is pushing a weighty encumbrance around the block; it won't take long for both partners to run out of energy and dump the marriage at the nearest divorce court.

6. Sexual and Marital Fidelity

It doesn't take a genius to admit how sex-crazy our society is. As bad as it is, however, adultery, fornication, homosexuality, and "dirty tapes and views" have always been around. Even in biblical times, people faced temptations that carried the potential to destroy healthy families. Apparently, God takes this sexual sin seriously because when sexual dysfunction, perversion, or infidelity sets into a marriage, the marriage is severely harmed. Some biblical scholars see sexual sin as the only grounds for a biblical divorce; if so, it makes faithfulness the single most important aspect in keeping marriages together. The Christian couple that desires a healthy relationship can't afford to neglect this area or to fall into the attitude that they are not susceptible. Both in biblical times and postmodern, there are plenty of men and women who are willing to forsake their own marriages or violate the marriage vows of someone else in order to selfishly find personal satisfaction. This destroys marriages.

Sexual fidelity is more than refraining from sexual intercourse with someone of the opposite gender other than a spouse. Emotional affairs can be just as disruptive and destructive to intimacy as full adultery. Jesus made lust of the heart equal to adultery (Matt. 5:28). In his view, even wanting someone (anyone) other than your own spouse is defined as adultery of the heart, and sexual fidelity in Scripture is serious business, not to be viewed apart from its devastating impact. One of the greatest gifts a child can be given is knowing that two parents remained faithful to each other throughout years of marriage. Where marital vows have been broken, God's grace is certainly sufficient to bring about healing, but the relationship will never be the same. The impact of adultery is forgivable but in many cases not repairable. It is for this reason God places a unique kind of judgment upon the breach of the marriage bed (1 Cor. 6:18; Heb. 13:4).

One the most interesting elements about doing research on contemporary family life is what I did *not* find. Because one can find a study to prove almost anything, I had assumed because of the sexually permissive society we live in there would be research to suggest that healthy families entertain open marriages or multiple affairs. I was pleasantly surprised. Not one credible study done on healthy families suggested that "alternative" sexual expressions within the marital bond were deemed healthy.[21] On the contrary, what is found is that the healthiest families have a high degree of religious orientation, commitment to traditional values, and monogamy.

In other words, what the Bible consistently says about the importance of sexual fidelity in marriage is in keeping with the literature on what constitutes healthy family relations. Healthy marriages do not flourish where couples are sexually permissive, experimenting, or fooling around.

7. Concern for the Larger World

This past year I was asked to speak at a church that had recently lost its pastor. After the service one of the leaders took me to lunch and explained that the church board had asked the pastor to leave because of his views concerning the Y2K problem. The pastor encouraged parishioners to sell their homes, move to Idaho, and create a community where they could stockpile food and other provisions. The leader asked me what I thought about it, and I replied, "Sounds like one sick puppy."

During the years leading up to the year 2000 I met several others who held similar concerns. In my opinion they had jettisoned their Christian concern for the larger world and adopted a selfish fortress mentality. As I understand the gospel, the only reason God has left us in this world is to bear witness to his love and grace. It seems much more difficult to give witness while living inside a compound in the woods.

God's concern for those not yet in his family and for those less fortunate is a consistent emphasis in Scripture.

As creator of all, God has made all humankind siblings. We share a common life. Those who follow the teaching of Jesus must look with compassion to those outside the doors of their own homes. Just as Israel had responsibility to care for those who passed through its borders and those who fell into need, so Christian families need to reach outside to the needs of their larger community. Families turned in on themselves are not at all healthy. Healthy families do not limit their caring and commitment, but allow their affections and actions to spill over into society.

Several years ago, while we were living in the Philadelphia suburbs, an event took place that shocked almost everyone in the city. On the very doorsteps of a Northeast Philly church a young teenager was beaten to death by several other youths using baseball bats. During the beating several members of households living across the street were dialing 911. Later, national news coverage spun the tragedy as a failure of Philly's 911 system. As I remember the details, some twenty different calls were made covering a period of nearly forty-five minutes. When I heard about it my thought was, *Where were the Christians in that neighborhood?* I can't imagine looking out my window and watching four or five bullies kick someone to death without going outside and yelling "STOP." I would grab the nearest weapon at hand—bat, golf club, or tire wrench—go across the street and risk injury to myself to stop the brutality. What has become of our country when we feel absolutely no responsibility beyond the confines of our own protected homes? If you don't know what you might have done in the same situation, ask yourself if the nature of your response changes when you see that the child being beaten is your own? Most mothers with a broomstick or kitchen knife would have been over there in an instant to protect their own son. What the episode illustrates is not the failure of the 911 system, but the failure of families to care about a world beyond their doorstep.

Clapp has suggested, "To be healthy, the family needs a mission or purpose beyond itself . . . the long and short of it is that we need a world bigger, richer, tougher than that which can be created by a little family fixated on itself and its emotional coddling."[22] Healthy families make one more place at the dinner table or throw a sleeping bag on the floor to accommodate a visitor. Our family celebrated this past Christmas at our married daughter's home. Around the Christmas tree, besides the members of our immediate family, were five teen-aged foster boys. Being a foster parent to one adolescent is difficult enough, but five? My daughter and her husband are doing what most parents won't do, and what I probably could not do. This is the heart of what a biblically healthy family is all about; after all, isn't Christmas about welcoming the one for whom no one else had room?[23]

Conclusion

The Mystery and the Mess*

Cinny and I started with energy, enthusiasm, and idealism. She swept me off my feet with romantic intensity. On the day of our wedding she was the most beautiful thing I had ever seen. (She still is!) Our first years together we moved from house to house with eager anticipation of better things. From the first year onward, we read books on marriage, attended couples' retreats, went to child-birth classes with pillows in hand, took days off just to be together, did family vacations, and tried to reach our neighbors for Christ. We held Bible studies in our home, sent the kids to Christian camps, taught Sunday school and marriage enrichment retreats. All this while I managed to complete two graduate degrees, work several jobs, and bathe the kids at night. Cinny did whatever she could to realize additional income for the family, care for whomever showed up on our doorstep, and get three children off to schools, music lessons, and sporting events. Money was usually tight, the house not quite big enough, the furniture was hand-me-downs or give-aways, and someone was always hungry, sick, or upset about something. Along the way people stepped into our lives from outside our family. Friends cared for our children when we went to Israel, relatives supported us financially, church members in comparable circumstances laughed with us about our joint plight, and some people of generous assets opened their homes and lives to us.

As I detail this reflection, I am thankful our family has not experienced the kinds of tragedy other families have faced. We had our share of aches and pains, but they are not on the same scale as those who have seen a spouse or children killed, raped, or suffer debilitating illnesses. Our pains have been the standard broken bones, flu bugs, bounced checks, and cars being towed away from no-parking-zones. Here we are, after thirty-plus years of marriage—together, somewhat sane, clothed, and hopefully in our right minds. But what has been most devastating to me is the loss of the romantic ideal about marriage and family. None of my kids went to Harvard, one barely made it through high school, and one is divorced. That's why I hate getting standard family Christmas letters and don't write them any more. So what does this loss of the romantic ideal represent about marriage and family life? Without asking the question, one will never know what lesson is to be learned. As Coontz says, "Nostalgia for traditional families, and myths about their strengths, prevent us from drawing useful lessons from the past and making effective innovations for our families' future."[1]

What giving up notions of nostalgia means is that with all my education and experience I failed to consider two critical aspects of a healthy family, suggested by a speaker I once heard: "What keeps screwing up everything is the mystery and mess."

The Mess We Are In

Romantic ideals are great. Romance is the stuff that makes for best-selling novels—and babies. Nothing great ever happens apart from some ideal. But as Bloom points out, "There is practically nothing within our horizon that can come to the aid of ideal longing." He continues, "Sure, you can be a romantic today if you so choose, but it is a little like being a virgin in a whorehouse. It just doesn't fit with the temper of the times and gets no support in the current atmosphere."[2] Romantic ideals about family life do not fit the times. What I have tried to demonstrate in this book is that they have never fit the times. Family ideals exist in both society and Scripture, but they are rarely lived out. Why?

Because of the mess! The mess is you, me, and everyone else in the world! Chuck Colson observes about this idea, "the most consistent empirical proof from history is the doctrine of human depravity." We have just finished the twentieth century and ushered in the twenty-first; what was the most common experience during the past century? Go into any large bookstores and browse the history section; what do you see? My rough guess would be that 80 percent of the titles on the shelf are on the subject of war. From a quick scan it would seem human history is substantially the history of warfare. Not a nice tribute to the human race, is it? But if we accept scriptural testimony, this history should not surprise us. You see what it is that keeps screwing up everything? It is the perversity and subtle deception of my own fallen heart.

The doctrine that God created humanity in his own image is the first axiom of biblical personhood. The human image expressed in diversity (male and female) constituted this divine image, designed to live in unity (Gen. 2:24). A plurality in the Godhead created a plurality in humanity (1:27). The relationship of maleness and femaleness was designed to experience a "one-flesh" intimacy, but the next verse says, "Now the serpent" (3:1). This first couple fell for a scheme, trading their human innocence for sinful knowledge. Cast out of the garden, ultimately they enjoyed the marvel of the first human birth. Cain, their firstborn son, must have been seen as a kind of redeemer or symbol of human renewal after the tragic failure of the parents (4:1).[3] As parents commonly have, Adam and Eve must have had ambitions and expectations for what their son's life would be. But their romantic notions about the future were shattered when Cain killed his brother Abel. (It was the first first-degree murder and the first human death.) With one child dead and the other banished for life, the first couple had to start over. They gave birth to Seth, who was the father of Enosh (4:25–26).

In Hebrew, Seth means "foundation." The verbal root for the name Enosh means "to be sick, weak, or have an incurable wound."[4] This may be a subtle way of introducing the theology of the "mess" to the reader. It is also at this point in history that "men began to call on the name of the Lord" (Gen. 4:26). Until our first parents recognized the incurable human wound, there was no need to call upon the Lord; this passage sets the stage for everything else in the Bible.

The prophet Jeremiah says "the heart is more deceitful than all else and is desperately sick; Who [then] can understand it?" (Jer. 17:9 NASB). This verse may be depressing, but a sense of encouragement comes from the next line: the Lord searches our minds and hearts and gives to us according to our ways. I'm not sure how encouraging it is that our hearts are searched by the Lord, but it does assure me that at least *someone* knows me. The passage teaches that no human being can understand his or her own heart, much less the heart of anyone else. I may think I know my wife, but I don't. She may think she knows me, but no way. There is more in my heart than she will ever know, and neither of us even knows ourselves completely. According to Jeremiah, realistic self-knowledge is impossible.

The second thing the Jeremiah passage says is that our own hearts lie to us! A deceitful heart is a heart that doesn't tell you the truth. I cannot trust my own heart because it is constantly lying to me. You see this is the kind of mess I inherited from my primary biological parents, Adam and Eve.

You may be asking, "Doesn't Jesus change all this?" What Jesus brings to our lives is a foretaste of what is yet to come, like the little samples offered at grocery stores and food courts in the malls. We are enticed by the aroma and taste of sesame chicken, but the petite bite leaves us wanting more. I would suggest that because in marriage we are dealing with two fallen human beings, the best we can ever do is achieve a foretaste on earth of true intimacy. The apostle Paul acknowledges that though we have the Spirit of God as the firstfruit (sample) of our redemption, we still "groan" with the creation for the time when we will be free from the present corruption. We wait in hope for the total freedom and adoption of sons and daughters of God (Rom. 8:20–25). This is the hope that does not disappoint (5:5). Apparently, Paul knew all other hopes would ultimately prove faulty.

What an understanding and appreciation of the mess does is move the romantic ideals of marriage and family to another plane—but not a lower plane as we might think. It is the plane of a costly, deathly reality, a plane where we must call upon the name of the Lord to save our marriages and our children. It is a plane that involves a cross instead of a happy face. It is a plane where we are asked to die with no hope of resurrection. After we have been disappointed by every element of family life and declared it dead, we are in a position to acknowledge the fatal wound resident in our hearts. Someone once observed that we must learn to mourn the death of our loved ones while they are still living. In this light, every family disillusionment or disappointment puts another nail in the coffin. Our frustrations and difficulties with a spouse or child become tears, and we mourn what we expected but did not receive.

You see, getting Dad to be the head of the home or asking Mom to play a certain role doesn't do a thing to change the reality of the mess. Even attempts to cultivate biblical responsibilities will fail or disappoint. Our expectations are too great, our need for intimacy greater than our spouse's abilities, and our hearts too fickle to find the bliss we desire on earth.

We must see ourselves as Enosh, weak, frail, and failing. Until we do, we probably won't call upon the Lord. Until we do, we will keep trying to fix marriages, parents, and children with Band-Aid solutions that leave us more angry and frustrated. As one writer notes, "Most troubled marriages are where both partners are working on too many things in their marriage and miss the 'one thing needed,'"[5] sitting at Jesus' feet (Luke 10:39, 41–42).

Because of the mess that is me I cannot promise my wife that she will always feel loved or that I will daily care for her in the ways she likes. Reality and human nature say otherwise. Mason observes, "A vow is per se, a confession of inadequacy and an automatic calling upon the only adequacy there is, which is the mercy and power of God."[6]

Perhaps God has brought me to the place he wants me. I am tired and disillusioned about much of what I have seen in my own home life and the home life of others. But I know where I am. I know my condition. That's why the little marital and parental appetizers that are thrown my way from time to time are so enjoyable. This past Labor Day weekend was one such tasteful experience. Two of our extended family members were in town so we held a cookout at our home for the rest of the family. Since some were house-sitting or baby-sitting other people's kids, we ended up with a houseful. After I finished barbecuing and made sure everyone got enough to eat, the children jumped into the pool, and I played the role of lifeguard. As I sat there drinking my cup of coffee and watching this collection of grandkids, friends, and relatives, I thought,

It just doesn't get any better than this. The children splashed, cannonballed, and Marco-Poloed. Little enclaves of adults discussed everything from concerns for a dying parent to what kind of season the Gators were going to have. As I looked at the three generations gathered there, I thought, *This is what family is all about.* It's not anything in particular that makes it a blessing; it's just that *it is.* Knowing that this is just a foretaste of heaven made me savor my Labor Day tidbit.

The Mystery That Is God in Me

Over the years Cinny and I have had the privilege of meeting all kinds of couples and families. Many of these have been married much longer than we have, some have divorced, some have significantly prospered, others barely make it financially. Time and experience offer fascinating perspectives on the history of some of these families. One couple that comes to mind is in their sixties, childhood sweethearts dating all through college and marrying upon graduation. The husband went into business, two kids followed, and through a local lay ministry husband and wife received Christ as their savior. After all these years, I still consider their marriage a model relationship. They are well-matched, close friends, and affectionate after some forty years of marriage. As far as I know they have been faithful to each other and their God. They have served their church and community, and have led many to Christ over the years. Yet, their two children did not follow their example or convictions. One recently died of a drug overdose and the other wants nothing to do with Christianity. So what happened? It's easy to speculate, but there are no answers that make sense.

Another husband and wife we know were raised in Christian homes and met in college through a campus ministry. They married and went into Christian service as their family expanded to seven with the birth of five children. Their house always seemed like Grand Central Station, somewhat chaotic, but always hospitable and enjoyable. The five children went to prestigious colleges, and from the perspective of Christians and non-Christians alike, have turned out superbly. So what was their secret to raising successful children? Again, it is easy to speculate but hard to pin down direct cause-and-effect relationships.

A third couple enters my mind at this point who met while teaching at the same school. After a short courtship they moved into a small house, produced two children, and struggled to make ends meet. After a decade of financial stress, alcohol abuse, and marital strife, the couple agreed to an amiable divorce. The wife gained custody of the two children and raised them virtually by herself. Both children graduated from college and have careers of their own. They adore their mother and are loving, spiritually minded, and gifted people, appreciative of the lives they have.

How did this single mother raise children without the support and love of a husband? Again, theories abound, but they all seem absurd. Take any couple's marriage, or any parenting dynamics—I believe it is impossible to derive hardcore cause-and-effect theory that fully explains success or failures. There are missing elements, anomalies, and exceptions that cannot be explained. It is this "mystery" element that fascinates me about family life.

We can put forth many rules, responsibilities, structures, helpful hints, and common traits of healthy families, but they are nothing more than dead paradigms. What is missing is what Walter Percy has called the "delta phenomenon." Using the story of Helen Keller and her teacher, he depicts this phenomenon as the time when Anne Sullivan is pouring "wet stuff" over the hand of blind and deaf Helen Keller while simultaneously signing W-A-T-E-R. The moment the symbols W-A-T-E-R make a connection with cold wet stuff running through Helen's fingers, the "delta phenomenon" occurs. No one really understands how the human mind makes the leap from unassociated symbols to language; we just know it happens. I contend the same is true of marriage and family life. The delta phenomenon takes place all the time in communication and emotional exchange; some things about marriage and family life are just too mysterious to understand.

The apostle Paul briefly alludes to the dynamic when he calls both the relationship of Christ to the church and the relationship of a man with a woman a mystery (Eph. 5:31–32). It's interesting how the idea is dropped between thoughts. Paul had been developing the responsibility of the husband in loving his wife and then goes on to quote Genesis 2:24 saying, "For this reason a man will leave his father and mother and be united to his wife, and they shall become one flesh." Out of the blue, he then says, "This is a profound mystery." What mystery? The mystery of how two opposites can become one! He then gives a final responsibility to the couple: "Each one of you also must love his wife as he loves himself, and the wife must respect her husband" (Eph. 5:33). Sandwiched between the responsibility sections, Paul acknowledges you can't fully understand the mystery. But Paul is not the only one to see family relationships through these eyes.

Agur writes, "There are things which are too wonderful (mysterious) for me, four which I do not understand: the way of an eagle in the sky, the way of serpent on a rock, the way of ship in the sea and the way of man with woman" (Prov. 30:18–19). Each of these illustrations reflects limitations to human logic, science, and knowledge. As a private pilot I enjoy flying. When a pilot obtains his preflight weather briefing, he also gets a status on bird activity around the runway. The report lists low, moderate, or high bird watch. Usually, at altitude, bird activity is less than at lower altitudes. But occasionally I have been at several thousand feet when I notice a hawk or seagull magically hanging in the air bouncing along with the currents of wind. I wonder, *Why is he so high and what is he doing up here? He can't be hunting, mating, or going somewhere.* With his wings fully extended I realize he is just riding the currents and apparently enjoying it.

I relate! Agur says this is the way it is between a man and a woman. Some couples rise to heights unfathomed. How they got there is a mystery. In the illustration, each of the subjects has its own unique environment (air, rock, sea, and marriage) and each go where there are no well-worn paths.[7] In marriage, every couple exists in their own unique environment, one that defies understanding and goes where no paths are cut. In this sense, each couple is a trailblazer living on the edge of new life frontiers. Their experience can't be followed or traced, and where they have been, even they are unable to describe. Such is the mystery of marriage.

Other proverbs take a deeper look into this mystery but do not offer a quick, consumer-ready, user-friendly approach to marriage and family life. What is offered is an evocative look at marriage rather than a pragmatic how-to approach. King Lemuel asks, "A wife of noble character who can find?" (Prov. 31:10). This rhetorical question poses the evocative and illusive nature of the relationship. It acknowledges that good wives exist, but are exceedingly rare. In addition, we are told "a wife of noble character is her husband's crown" (12:4). This merely affirms what a good wife is to her husband, no more or less. There are no lists or helpful hints given about how to be a crown to the husband, or how the husband can improve the crownship of his wife. Just the simple reality.

The closest Proverbs comes to suggesting how one can find a good wife is: "Houses and wealth are inherited from parents, but a prudent wife is from the Lord" (Prov. 19:14).

The second part of the verse is not clear. Does it mean a good wife is an unexpected, unsought gift? Again, we are left with the intriguing mystery about marriage and the finding of a good mate.

Proverbs depicts the opposite reality as well. Some marriages are characterized by contention, strife, and "dripping" annoyances (21:9; 25:24; 27:15–16). The long-term effect of such things is "decay in his bones" (12:4). Again, the sage who wrote the Proverbs does not offer any more insight than the fact that some marriages can destroy the life of an individual. No marriage therapy exists here, no "fixes" for the dysfunctional relationship, just the quiet, unashamed reality that both kinds of marriages exist. Some marriages wear crowns. Others rot. An explanation for either kind of these marriages is left to the reader. Some families are like soaring seagulls, others like leaky faucets. Someone once said, "He who gets a good wife thanks the Lord; he who gets a bad wife becomes a philosopher." I am still thanking the Lord!

In the final analysis, two streams of family reality merge to form a mystery. Solomon apparently studied human life as much as any man alive in his day. He had the wealth, time, and inclination to make it an ongoing pursuit (Eccles. 1:13). If anything, the conclusion from his research is pessimistic. Having experienced everything that claimed to offer satisfaction (sex, wealth, folly, women, massive construction projects) he concluded that all of them failed to deliver on their claim. "Vanity of vanity," says the preacher; that's his conclusion about life. Yet, the explanation for Solomon's conclusion is revealing. He explains that God "has made everything beautiful in its time. He has also set eternity in the hearts of men; yet they cannot fathom what God has done from beginning to end" (3:11). Our creator has woven eternity into our hearts for the specific purpose that we will not be able to know what God is doing in our lives. We are bound by our own human limitations while our eternal nature longs for satisfaction, intimacy, and understanding. Apparently, to have the kind of relationship we really desire, it takes infinite understanding and knowledge. It takes God! Apart from God or with God, life is a mystery!

Solomon acknowledges there is little rhyme or reason to the complexity of human enterprise. "The race is not to the swift or the battle to the strong, nor does food come to the wise or wealth to the brilliant or favor to the learned; but time and chance happen to them all" (Eccles. 9:11). In other words, the fastest runner doesn't necessarily win the race. The best army may not win the battle; the Harvard graduate may end up poor and broke. A person can do all the right things and not be rewarded, honored, or compensated. It means in marriage, there are no guarantees. It means a couple can live godly lives and still have children who reject the Lord. It means non-Christian couples may have better marriages than some Christians. It means all our family relationships are unpredictable and uncertain. From our limited earthly viewpoint, "under the sun," life is mysterious. Only God knows what is really going on in anyone's life, and unfortunately, he rarely lets us know.

"Enjoy life with the woman whom you love all the days of your fleeting life which he has given to you under the sun," concludes Solomon, "for this is your lot in life and in your toilsome labor under the sun" (Eccles. 9:9). This is wisdom stripped of all superficiality, pious platitudes, and role-playing. When push comes to shove it all comes down to this: No matter where we are on our family journey, we have limited time. Family life is about loving—nothing more, nothing less. Because of the mystery of family life, we don't know how much time God will allow us to have with any of our loved ones, but the only reward in this life is the reward of our relationships. If we genuinely care about our spouse, children, grandchildren, or great-grandchildren, we will seize the days we have with them. My life is fleeting and so is theirs! The wisdom of God dictates enjoying relationships while I can. Enjoying life with the people you love is what family life is all about. No; it is what *life* is about.

An aging Anglican priest sat in his favorite lounge chair enjoying his book when his teenage grandson bolted through the front door of the rectory. The young man blurted out, "Granddad, I'm in love." The priest slowly put down his reading material, rose to his feet, and embraced his grandson. He then took his arm and said, "Help me upstairs." The two took the stairs slowly and finally reached the second floor where a hallway led to a bedroom. The pulsating sounds of a respirator echoed off the unadorned walls. "Come in and sit down for a moment," said the old priest. The young man took a seat at the foot of the bed and waited. His grandfather slipped next to a figure reclining in the bed and gently took the IV-laced wrinkled hand of his wife. "My son, this is love!" he whispered.

Afterword

In a publishers' meeting discussing my "philosophy of writing," I illuminated what makes Bob Hicks tick, for whom I was trying to write, and my manner of book development. Then someone asked, "It seems to me you never ask your readers to do anything." Actually, this was a statement not a question, but I knew the individual was looking for an answer, so I gave him one.

I replied, "I don't ask them to do anything because I don't want them to *do* anything."

Since this discussion was centered on one of my men's books, I added, "I want men to better understand themselves, not *do* something. If anything, men are such compulsive doers, they often do not have a clue about how they feel or even why they are doing what they're doing. My goal in writing is to get them to take some time to understand what it is they are doing and help them get in touch with how they feel about it."

By the looks on the faces around the table, I quickly concluded the publishing representatives were not impressed by my honesty or my philosophy. In fact, what they really wanted was for me to change how I wrote, how I approach men, and to ask the readers to do something . . . anything!

Do I want you, my reader, to *do* something?

Miracle of miracles, I do. Hopefully, this book has demonstrated that attempts to identify the perfect family are a misleading, exhausting, and futile pursuit. There are no perfect families to be found, none to follow, and not one to admire from a distance. There are only families like yours and mine. If your family sometimes fights, sometimes is frustrated with each other, fearful of children's futures, financially weary and depressed, then guess what? You fit the biblical models of family life! Better yet, you are a prime candidate for divine intervention and grace.

So what is it I am asking you to do? That's simple. Give up the compulsive search for the phantom ideal. We cannot truly embrace the families we have until we burn in effigy the myth of the perfect family. Comparing our failures to some ideal relationships (whatever model we might have) only breeds dissatisfaction with those we have, so give it up!

The second thing I want you to do is to embrace and seek enjoyment in the family relationships God has given you. This means accepting your family the way they are. When I teach this to my students and listeners, sometimes they draw a faulty conclusion. When they hear "give up your ideal family myth" they mistakenly hear "there is nothing one can do to make a relationship better, so don't even try!" This is an erroneous assumption. I believe most relationships can be made better. But we have to ask, by what? In whose timing? By whom? At what cost in terms of energy, emotion, and difficulties created in other areas? You see, we must entertain an equal possibility that in trying to make something better, we in fact can make it worse. As pragmatic, ever-optimistic-about-everything Americans, this goes vigorously against the grain of our cultural psyches. Why do we always think we can make something better just by doing something?[1]

Yes, the possibility always exists that our relationships can be made better. That's why biblical imperatives, exhortations, prohibitions, and admonitions are given. From Moses to the apostles, instruction is offered to regulate family living. The assumption is always present that in so doing, these relations will be made better. However, never forget these commands and prohibitions exist simply because Israelites and Christians were having serious problems in their families. The divine counsel is given to be therapeutic in the context of family confusion, strife, and discord. "Biblical" families were not perfect. Fallen spouses, parents, and children stand in need of God's grace and counsel. If anything, the counsel Scripture provides helps us to better understand how this God of grace hangs in there with us. It shows us how to continue loving, forgiving, and accepting the fallen creatures God has placed into our families. I believe it is this irrational and unconditional acceptance over time (God's timing) that brings about changes in human beings and families.

Fundamentally, I don't believe one human being can bring about significant developmental changes in another human being (especially adults). We can teach basic educational content and instill discipline while we have supervisory control. But conformity is a mere behavioral cosmetic. Once a person is on his own and confronts the trials and pressures of life, he reveals who he really is. The apostle Paul makes this very clear in Romans 5:1–5 where he shatters the illusions of our human hopes. He argues the only hope that does not disappoint over time is the hope that emerges as a result of tribulation and distress.[2] This hope, born in the afflictions of life, produces "proven character." We would like to think of character as something that can be produced in the lives of our kids, spouses, disciples, or ourselves, but both Paul and James affirm that character only comes from tough times. In other words, there is no true character without tribulation. Without the external stressors life throws at us, character is only unproven personality.

The hope that does not disappoint is the "hope of the glory of God" (Rom. 5:2). Peter calls this a "living hope" (as opposed to the dead hopes we place in humans). It is God upon whom we are to "fix our hope" completely. Our hope is rooted in the grace of God to be revealed at the revelation of Jesus Christ when he comes to take us home (1 Peter 1:3, 13). It is the only hope that outlasts all human disappointments, changes people, and proves character.

The only way we can change another human being is by changing ourselves and our responses to what is going on in our lives. The simple reason for this is that we only have true control over ourselves, and we can't change what we can't control! If I can't control the circumstances, at least I can control my attitudes and responses to the circumstances.

Marriage and family life is far messier and more mysterious than I ever dreamed. I can't put it in a neat little box colorfully wrapped with attractive ribbons. All I can do is seek to live it and embrace it day by day!

So what does this mean? I believe families always have the hope of change and building better relationships. But how are they made better? We have been led to believe that such things as marriage seminars, family conferences, books, tapes, and family therapy are all keys to building happier families. I have personally found all these resources helpful to my marriage and family, yet they have not necessarily made me a better person or a more godly man. At the end of the seminar or counseling session, I am still the same Bob Hicks going back to the same set of circumstances and people. I still have the same personality, the same sensitivities I find hard to talk about, the same in-laws, children, wife, and yard that needs mowing. Some days when I think about what it is I have to face, I am ready to bail out or just go back to bed. Focusing on the family is not enough. The writer of Hebrews tells us that we are to "fix our eyes upon Jesus, who is the author and perfecter of our faith" (Heb. 12:2). But when I think of Christ and the uncertain brevity of life facing all of us, it makes me want to kiss my wife, tell my kids how much I love them, and take my grandkids on a date.

Biblical love is not a gushy emotion or sympathy of spirits. As Leon Morris says, "We cannot assume that the way we use the word love in a modern western community is the way it was used in the Bible."[3] In the New Testament, love (agape) is characterized by action, as in "for God so loved the world that he gave . . ." (John 3:16). Paul's extended discourse on love defines love with only two attributes: kindness and patience (1 Cor. 13:4), throwback concepts to the patient lovingkindness of God in the Old Testament (see Ps. 62:12; Jer. 31:3). Morris calls it "the love that will not let us go, the love that not all man's weakness and sinfulness and stubbornness can destroy."[4]

What is real in terms of God's love for us becomes the ideal to strive for in our fallen human relationships. The rest of Paul's love passage merely outlines how this love is not characterized (it is not arrogant, jealous, or bragging) and concludes with the kind of actions love performs (bears all things, believes all things, hopes all things, endures all things).

So, give up the search for the perfect family and love the people in your life with all their faults, quirks, irritations, temper tantrums, melancholic moods, and rebellion. Put up with them the way Christ puts up with you.

Reach out and grab the one with whom you're disenchanted or disappointed. Find something positive, affirming, or accepting to say or do for them. Don't expect any preconceived return on your action. Just accept them where they are and whatever their reaction. If relationships are changed for the better, that is most likely to happen in the spirit of contentment, not disappointment.

The apostle Paul says it is this kind of love that "never fails" (1 Cor. 13:8) and makes everything else possible. Love fulfills the entirety of biblical instructions and everything those principles are meant to accomplish. "Therefore love is the fulfillment of the law" (Rom. 13:10).

Notes

Preface

1. Researchers at the University of Chicago say the number of married couples with children dropped from 45 percent in the early '70s to 26 percent in 1998. Two-parent single-earner families with children are now the exception rather than the rule. Only 56 percent of adults are married compared to 75 percent in the '70s. Only half of today's children live with two parents or stepparents in the same household. The number of unmarried couples living together is up to 33 percent, more than doubling [*The New York Times,* 26 November 1999].

2. The Greek term, *oikourous,* means house-worker.

Chapter 1

1. He is in a Movie and Television Production program at a local media school. Their philosophy is "Real World Education," which means required studio time, working the kind of schedule the media business works. Film and recording studios are sometimes only available during the early morning hours.

2. See George Barna, *The Future of the American Family* (Chicago: Moody Press, 1993), 25–38, 178, where he contrasts the "traditional family" with the "nouveau family."

3. See James Dobson and Gary Bauer, *Children at Risk: The Battle for the Hearts and Minds of Our Kids* (Dallas: Word, 1990), 112, for the debate on the use of statistics in defining) "traditional family."

4. Judith Wallerstein's latest work, *The Unexpected Legacy of Divorce* (New York: Hyperion, 2000) claims married couples with children represent 26 percent of American households. Review of book quoted in *USA Today,* "Unhappily Ever After," September 5, 2000.

5. Statistics published in *The New York Times,* 15 May 2001, "For First Time, Nuclear Families Drop Below 25% of Households," p. A1.

6. Ibid.

7. Nice sounding phrases which in reality mean "you've been fired."

Chapter 2

1. Rodney Clapp, *Families at the Crossroads: Beyond Traditional & Modern Options* (Downer's Grove, Ill.: InterVarsity Press, 1993), 28–29.

2. Today Raytheon owns Beech. Walter Beech paid my dad in cash out of his own pocket during the early days. Dad worked at Travel Air and then Beech for forty-three years.

3. Walter Beech sent my dad to business school at night to study accounting. The last thing my dad did before he died in January 1993 at the age of 83 was finish his tax return. I still usually do mine on April 14 and need lots of help. So much for higher education!

4. Dr. Ben is still my mother's physician and still considered "family."

5. Walter Beech's wife, Olive Ann, who had been my dad's first secretary, eventually took over the company as president and CEO when Walter died.

6. Having raised teenagers of my own, I realize now my father may have had other reasons for not being home more.

7. See William J. Lederer and Don D. Jackson, *The Mirages of Marriage* (New York: W.W. Norton & Co., 1968), 41–84 for a discussion of "marital myths" or "mirages" as they call them.

8. Frances and Joseph Gies, *Marriage and the Family in the Middle Ages* (New York: Harper & Row, 1987), 4.

9. See "The Late Medieval Peasant Family: 1350–1500," *Marriage and the Family,* 235–50.

10. John Demos, *Past, Present and Personal: The Family and the Life Course in American History* (New York: Oxford University Press, 1986), x.

11. Stephanie Coontz, *The Way We Never Were: American Families and the Nostalgia Trap* (New York: HarperCollins, 1992), 11.

12. Michael D. Richards and Paul R. Waibel, *Twentieth Century Europe: A Brief History* (Wheeling: Harlan Davidson, Inc., 1999), 14.

13. Ibid., 13.

14. Demos, *Past, Present and Personal,* 12. He adds, "Hysteria, neurathenia, breakdown; whatever the favored diagnostic category, their symptoms reflected strikingly on their life-situation."

15. Ibid., 76.

16. Ibid., 27.

17. John Demos, *A Little Commonwealth: Family Life in Plymouth Colony* (New York: Oxford University Press, 1970), 183.

18. See William A. Alcott, *The Young Wife* (1837).

19. Demos, *A Little Commonwealth,* 28.

20. Sydney E. Ahlstrom, *A Religious History of the American People* (New Haven, Yale University Press, 1972), 146.

21. Ibid., 151.

22. Samuel Eliot Morison, *The Oxford History of the American People* (New York, Oxford University Press, 1965), 66.

23. Demos, 128.

24. Research by Coontz (*The Way We Never Were,* 73) claims that Laura Ingalls' original memoirs were rewritten by her daughter as "an ideological attack" on

government programs. In the rewrites, the Ingallses are an isolated family pitted against the elements with no help from the community. The original memoirs record otherwise; in fact, they infer large government subsidies.

25. My father's family homesteaded in Douglas County, Missouri. It was from this farm that my father with his parents moved to Wichita, Kansas.

26. Craig Miner, ed., *The Wichita Reader: A Collection of Writings About a Prairie City* (Wichita: The Wichita Eagle and Beacon Publishing Co., 1992), 14.

27. Patricia Nelson Limerick, *Legacy of Conquest: The Unbroken Past of the American West* (New York: Norton, 1987), 82.

28. Glen Elder, *Children of the Great Depression: Social Change in Life Experience* (Chicago: University of Chicago Press), 64–82.

29. Dobson and Bauer, *Children at Risk,* 109.

30. Elaine Tyler May, *Homeward Bound: American Families in the Cold War Era* (New York: Basic Books, 1988), 11.

31. Ibid., 64.

32. Hollywood Story, "Laurin Chapin," aired on the *E Channel,* week of August 14–18, 2000.

33. Coontz, *The Way We Never Were,* 31.

34. Benita Eilser, *Private Lives: Men and Women of the Fifties* (New York: Franklin Watts, 1986), 341.

35. My good friend and literary agent Steve Griffith, a radical dog-lover, has suggested writing a book along these lines titled, "Raising Dogs God's Way."

36. While doing my doctoral work, I tried to find literature on family life from this early fundamentalist period. The literature was scant to nonexistent!

37. See the author's doctoral dissertation, "The Healthy Family: A Biblical and Sociological Evaluation and Proposed Model for Building Healthy Families in the Church" (Dallas Theological Seminary, 1988).

38. A "Psycho-Heresy" Ministry exists on the Internet that finds its purpose in "exposing" the false doctrine of people like Jim Dobson and me.

39. *The Masculine Journey* has been called "Psycho-heresy" by the same group that condemns Dobson.

40. Cal Thomas and Ed Dobson, ed., *Blinded by Might: Can the Religious Right Save America?* (Grand Rapids: Zondervan, 1999), 274.

41. See the books on the "Psycho-Heresy" of Jim Dobson. They include my writings as well.

42. James Dobson, *The Strong Willed Child: Birth through Adolescence,* 256–57. In *On Parenting.*

43. James Dobson, *New Dare to Discipline* (Wheaton, Ill: Tyndale House Publishers, 1992), 16.

44. The "underpinnings" include: Respect for parents; communication after discipline; control without nagging; not saturating the child with materialism; and balance between love and discipline, 18–48.

45. Ibid., 250.

46. Penelope Leach, *Children First: What Society Must Do—and Is Not Doing—for Children Today* (New York: Knopf, 1994).

47. Gies, *Marriage and the Family,* 11, 291.

48. Edward Shorter, *The Making of the Modern Family* (New York: Basic Books, 1975), 168–204.

49. Clapp, *Families at the Crossroads,* 13.

50. Web site article, "The Promise Keepers are Coming: The Third Wave of the Religious Right," Center for Democracy Studies, page 2. The article claims that the Promise Keepers organization has political connections and ambitions with James Dobson, Bill Bright, and Pat Robertson, all members of the religious right. The article leans to the left on social issues so it is not surprising they find fault with the religious right. See also Michael Barone, "Dobson's Choice," *National Review,* 20 April 1998.

51. Dobson and Bauer, *Children at Risk,* 28,32.

52. Ibid., 89.

53. Ibid., 41.

54. Thomas and Dobson, *Blinded by Might,* 118.

55. Paul Johnson, *A History of Christianity* (New York: Atheneum, 1985), 478–86.

56. The emperor of Rome was probably Nero at the time of Paul's writing. He was not exactly Christian, or family-values-friendly. He was probably a bisexual polygamist, who enjoyed torching Christians to light his garden.

57. In Thomas and Dobson, *Blinded by Might,* 80.

Chapter 3

1. See J. C. Wynn, *The Family Therapist* (Grand Rapids: Fleming H. Revell, 1987), for a good overview of various family system therapy approaches.

2. *Webster's Ninth New Collegiate Dictionary,* 1021.

3. Quoted in *The Promise Keepers Watch,* Online Edition, Center for Democracy Studies, No. 2-Special Supplement, 1997.

4. Quoted in Susan Faludi, *Stiffed: The Betrayal of the American Man* (New York: William Morrow and Company, 1999), 230.

5. Quoted in Al Janssen and Larry K. Weeden, eds., *Seven Promises of a Promise Keeper* (Colorado Springs: Focus on the Family Press, 1994),

6. See Nancy Groom, *Heart to Heart about Men* (Colorado Springs: NavPress, 1995) for the results of the research. NavPress went ahead and published the book without the Promise Keepers imprint or involvement.

7. Faludi, *Stiffed,* 236.

8. Ibid., 261. Faludi has given a fairly objective look at some of the Promise Keepers groups in her book. Though not a Christian, she does a good job detailing the pain, frustrations, and encouragements of a group of Promise Keepers.

9. William F. Arndt and F. Wilbur Gingrich, *A Greek-English Lexicon of the New Testament and Other Christian Literature* (Chicago: University of Chicago Press, 1957), 431.

10. Gilbert Bilezikian, *Beyond Sex Roles: A Guide for the Study of Female Roles in the Bible* (Grand Rapids: Baker, 1985), 161.

11. Arndt and Gingrich, *A Greek-English Lexicon,* 278.

12. Ibid, 560.

13. The Greek word *prosecho,* translated "manage," is the most general term for leadership. It basically has the idea of general oversight, paying attention to something, or caring for something. It probably does not include the nuts and bolts or details of management. Ibid, 721.

14. Wini Breines and Linda Gordon, "The New Scholarship on Family Violence," *Signs* 8 (1983).

15. Coontz, *The Way We Never Were,* 209–10.

16. See John Bradshaw, *Homecoming: Reclaiming and Championing Your Inner Child* (New York: Bantam Books, 1990).

17. Judith Rich Harris, *The Nurture Assumption* (New York: Free Press, 1998), 351.

18. Ibid., 361–62.

19. Arlene Skolnick, "The Myth of the Vulnerable Child," *Psychology Today,* 11 (1978): 58.

20. See my book, *In Search of Wisdom* an overview of the Book of Proverbs, where I develop these ideas in more detail.

21. Clapp, *Families at the Crossroads,* 142.

22. Frances Brown, S. R. Driver, and Charles A. Briggs, *A Hebrew and English Lexicon of the Old Testament* (London: Oxford University Press, 1972), 1046.

23. Colin Brown, ed., *The International Dictionary of New Testament Theology,* Vol. 3 (Grand Rapids: Zondervan, 1971), 71.

24. Gerhard Kittel and Gerhard Friedrich, *Theological Dictionary of the New Testament,* Vol. V(Grand Rapids: Eerdmans, 1976), 1016.

25. The section is also found in the other synoptic Gospels: Matt. 12 and Luke 8.

26. Clapp, *Families at the Crossroads,* 67–68.

Chapter 4

1. Gordon D. Kaufman, *An Essay on Theological Method* (Atlanta: Scholars Press, 1995), 3.

2. In ancient societies, seeing one's father naked was a breach of family ethics.

3. John J. Davis, *Paradise to Prison: Studies in Genesis* (Grand Rapids: Baker, 1975), 155.

4. Gary Smalley and John Trent, *The Blessing* (Nashville: Thomas Nelson, 1986), 17.

5. Derek Kidner, *Proverbs,* TOTC (Chicago: InterVarsity Press, 1964), 22.

6. Some try to argue a doctrine of racial purity from these texts, but my personal opinion is that the racial element was subservient to the idea of "spiritual purity." The concern was not racial but marrying someone of another faith who may compromise belief in the true God, Yahweh.

7. Hans Walter Wolff, *Anthropology of the Old Testament* (Philadelphia: Fortress Press, 1974), 182.

Chapter 5

1. Hazen G. Werner, *The Bible and the Family,* 64.

2. See Donald Guthrie, *New Testament Introduction* (Downer's Grove, Ill.: Inter-Varsity Press, 1990), for a concise and excellent treatment of the various positions.

3. Stephen Clark, *Man and Woman in Christ* (Ann Arbor: Servant Books, 1980), 87.

4. Mike Mason, *The Mystery of Marriage* (Portland: Multnomah Press, 1985), 147.

5. Guthrie, *New Testament Introduction*, 949.

6. Personally, I don't think Paul is the author. The language, structure, and type of argumentation are not characteristic of Paul.

7. Fritz Rienecker, *A Linguistic Key to the Greek New Testament*, 2 vols. (Grand Rapids: Zondervan, 1980), 2:372.

8. Alan Stibbs, *The First Epistle General of Peter* (Grand Rapids: Eerdmans, 1959), 127.

9. See Deborah Tannen's best-seller, *You Just Don't Understand: Women and Men in Conversation* (New York: Ballantine, 1990).

10. Clapp, *Families at the Crossroads*, 89.

11. *The Family: Preserving America's Future*, A Report to the President from the White House Working Group on the Family, United States Department of Education, Washington, D.C. p. 7.

12. Clapp, *Families at the Crossroads*, 144.

13. David Kantor and William Lehr, *Inside the Family* (San Francisco: Jossey-Bass, 1975), 49–50.

14. This proverb assumes a father who is "crazy" about his son. God deals with us in the same manner as a father who "delights in his son."

15. Nick Stinnett and John Defrain, *Secrets of Strong Families* (Boston: Little, Brown and Company, 1985), 17.

16. Urie Bronfenbrenner, *The American Family*, Audiotape, Harvard Seminar Series, 1981.

17. Mason, *Mystery of Marriage*, 28.

18. Interview with Jerry Falwell by Cal Thomas, quoted in *Blinded by Might*, 275.

19. Ibid., 259.

20. I do not have a problem with writing letters to congressmen and such. I maintain both my state senators and congressmen on my e-mail directory. But when I write them I am expressing my concerns as a responsible citizen of a free democratic society, and not looking to them to be the savior of our country. Our country exists by God's grace, and it will survive only through his continued undeserved favor!

21. Secular studies usually don't use evangelical terminology. Therefore "religious people" are said to hold "significant transcendent values." Of course, the "transcendent values" they talk about are "belief in God, going to church, and being sexually monogamous." See the classic Timberlawn study for reference: Jerry M. Lewis, W. Robert Beavers, J. T. Gossett, and V. A. Phillips, *No Single Thread: Psychological Health in Family Systems* (Philadephia: Brunner-Routledge, 1976).

22. Clapp, *Families at the Crossroads,* 164, 165.

23. Much of the biblical material in this chapter was taken from the author's doctoral dissertation, "The Healthy Family."

Conclusion

1. Coontz, *The Way We Never Were,* 281.

2. Allan Bloom, *Love and Friendship* (New York: Simon & Schuster, 1993), 25.

3. The phrase "I have gotten a manchild with the help of the Lord" can also be translated, "I have gotten a man, the Lord."

4. Brown, Driver, and Briggs, *Hebrew and English Lexicon of the Old Testament,* 60.

5. Mason, *The Mystery of Marriage,* 99.

6. Ibid., 94.

7. Sid Buzzell, *The Bible Knowledge Commentary,* Old Testament, 970.

Afterword

1. The Australians I know are not so optimistic. They have sometimes reminded me that there are greater possibilities for things going wrong in life and marriage than for things going right. Sometimes "doing the right thing" (Aussie slang) is doing nothing.

2. See Arndt and Gingrich for word studies on *thliphis,* "tribulation," defined as "distress brought on by outward circumstances," 363; and *dokimen,* "character," defined as "the quality of being approved, tested, " 201.

3. Leon Morris, *Testaments of Love: A Study of Love in the Bible* (Grand Rapids: Eerdmans, 1981), 3.

4. Ibid., 84.

Bibliography

Ahlstrom, Sydney E. *A Religious History of the American People.* New Haven: Yale University Press, 1972.

Arndt, William F. and F. Wilbur Gingrich. *A Greek-English Lexicon of the New Testament and Other Christian Literature.* Chicago: University of Chicago Press, 1957.

Barna, George. *The Future of the American Family.* Chicago: Moody Press, 1993.

Bilezikian, Gilbert. *Beyond Sex Roles: A Guide for the Study of Female Roles in the Bible.* Grand Rapids: Baker, 1985.

Bloom, Allan. *Love & Friendship.* New York: Simon & Schuster, 1993.

Bradshaw, John. *Homecoming: Reclaiming and Championing Your Inner Child.* New York: Bantam Books, 1990.

Breines, Wini and Linda Gordon. "The New Scholarship on Family Violence." *Signs* 8 (1983).

Brown, Colin, Editor. *The New International Dictionary of New Testament Theology,* 3 Volumes. Grand Rapids: Zondervan, 1971.

Brown, Frances, S. R. Driver, and Charles A. Briggs. *A Hebrew and English Lexicon of The Old Testament.* London: Oxford University Press, 1972.

Camm, Maurice. *The Jewish Way in Love & Marriage.* San Francisco: Harper & Row, 1980.

Clapp, Rodney. *Families at the Crossroads: Beyond Traditional & Modern Options.* Downers Grove: InterVarsity Press, 1993.

Clark, Stephen B. *Man and Woman in Christ.* Ann Arbor: Servant Books, 1980.

Coontz, Stephanie. *The Way We Never Were: American Families and the Nostalgia Trap.* New York: Harper Collins, 1992.

Demos, John. *A Little Commonwealth: Family Life in Plymouth Colony.* New York: Oxford University Press, 1970.

———. *Past, Present and Personal: The Family and the Life Course in American History.* New York: Oxford University Press, 1986.

Dobson, James and Gary L. Bauer. *Children at Risk: The Battle for the Hearts and Minds of Our Kids.* Dallas: Word, 1990.

Dobson, James. *Dr. James Dobson on Parenting: The Strong-Willed Child and Parenting Isn't for Cowards.* New York: Inspiration Press, 1997.

Dunn, Judy and Robert Plomin. *Separate Lives: Why Siblings Are So Different.* New York: Basic Books, 1991.

Eisler, Benita. *Private Lives: Men and Women in the Fifties.* New York: Franklin Watts, 1986.

Elder, Glen Jr. *Children of the Great Depression: Social Change in Life Experience.* Chicago: University of Chicago Press, 1974.

Faludi, Susan. *Stiffed: The Betrayal of the American Man.* New York: William Morrow and Company, 1999.

The Family: Preserving America's Future. A Report to the President from the White House Working Group on the Family. Family Research Council, 1986.

Forward, Susan and Craig Buck. *Toxic Parents: Overcoming Their Hurtful Legacy and Reclaiming Your Life.* New York: Bantam Books, 1989.

Gies, Frances and Joseph Gies. *Marriage and the Family in the Middle Ages.* New York: Harper & Row, 1987.

Gittelsohn, Roland B. *The Extra Dimension: A Jewish View of Marriage.* New York: Union of American Hebrew Congregations, 1983.

Goleman, Daniel. "Older Men and Happiness." *New York Times,* 24 February 1990.

Groom, Nancy. *Heart to Heart about Men.* Colorado Springs: NavPress, 1995.

Hicks, Robert M. *In Search of Wisdom.* Colorado Springs: NavPress, 1995.

———. *The Healthy Family: A Biblical and Sociological Evaluation and Proposed Model for Building Healthy Families in the Church.* Doctoral dissertation, Dallas Theological Seminary, 1988.

———. *The Masculine Journey.* Colorado Springs: NavPress, 1993.

Janssen, Al and Larry K. Weeden, eds. *Seven Promises of a Promise Keeper.* Colorado Springs: Focus on the Family Press, 1994.

Johnson, Paul. *A History of Christianity.* New York: Atheneum, 1985.

Kittel, Gerhard and Gerhard Friedrich. *Theological Dictionary of the New Testament,* 10 vol. Grand Rapids: Eerdmans, 1976.

Latourette, Kenneth Scott. *A History of Christianity.* New York: Harper & Row, 1953.

Lederer, William J. and Don D. Jackson. *The Mirages of Marriage.* New York: W.W. Norton & Co., 1968.

Lewine, Richard. "Parents: The Mental Health Professionals' Scapegoat." In *Changing Families,* edited by Irving Sigel and Luis Laosa. New York: Plenun, 1983.

Limerick, Patricia Nelson. *Legacy of Conquest: The Unbroken Past of the American West.* New York: Norton, 1987.

May, Elaine Tyler. *Homeward Bound: American Families in the Cold War.* New York: Basic Books, 1988.

Mason, Mike. *The Mystery of Marriage.* Portland: Multnomah Press, 1985.

McCartney, Bill. *What Makes a Man?* Colorado Springs: NavPress, 1992.

McCullough, Donald W. *The Trivialization of God: The Dangerous Illusion of a Manageable Deity.* Colorado Springs: NavPress, 1995.

Miner, Craig, ed. *The Wichita Reader: A Collection of Writing about a Prairie City.* Wichita: The Wichita Eagle and Beacon Publishing Co., 1992.

Morison, Samuel Eliot. *The Oxford History of the American People.* New York: Oxford University Press, 1965.

Morris, Leon. *Testaments of Love: A Study of Love in the Bible.* Grand Rapids: Eerdmans, 1981.

Orthner, Dennis. "The Family in Transition." In *Rebuilding the Nest: A New Commitment to the American Family.* Milwaukee: Family Service America, 1990.

Richards, Michael D. and Paul R. Waibel. *Twentieth-Century Europe: A Brief History.* Wheeling: Harlan Davidson, 1999.

Skolnick, Arlene. "The American Family: The Paradox of Perfection." *The Wilson Quarterly,* summer 1980.

———. "The Vulnerable Child." *Journal of Interdisciplinary History* 4 (1975).

Scott, George Ryley. *Curious Customs of Sex & Marriage.* London: The Guernsey Press, 1995.

Stinnett, Nick and John Defrain. *Secrets of Strong Families.* Boston: Little, Brown and Company, 1985.

Tannen, Deborah. *You Just Don't Understand: Women and Men in Conversation.* New York: Ballantine, 1990.

Thomas, Cal and Dobson, Ed. *Blinded by Might: Can the Religious Right Save America?,* Grand Rapids: Zondervan, 1999.

Tough, Allen. *Intentional Changes: A Fresh Approach to Helping People Change.* Chicago: Follet Publishing, 1982.

Walwoord, John F. and Roy B. Zuck. *The Bible Knowledge Commentary.* New Testament ed. Wheaton: Victor Books, 1983.

Wynn, J. C. *The Family Therapist.* Grand Rapids: Fleming H. Revell, 1987.

Dr. Robert Hicks resides in Montgomery, Alabama, where he is director of Chaplain services for the USAF Civil Air Patrol, as well as a freelance writer and adjunct professor of pastoral studies and history. He holds degrees in psychology, theology, and public administration. Author of two best-sellers, *The Masculine Journey* and *Uneasy Manhood,* Dr. Hicks enjoys reading, killing weeds, "dating" his granddaughters, and being a private pilot.